The Effective
Bank Supervisor

The Effective Bank Supervisor

HOW TO DEVELOP MANAGEMENT SKILLS

Paul F. Jannott

Bankers Publishing Company • Boston

Copyright © 1979 by
Bankers Publishing Company
210 South Street, Boston, Massachusetts 02111

Printed in the United States of America

Library of Congress Cataloging in Publication Data

Jannott, Paul F
    The effective bank supervisor

    1. Bank management. 2. Banks and banking—
Personnel management. I. Title.
HG1615.J35   658.3'7'3321   78-10579
ISBN 0-87267-030-9

Contents

Preface

This book is dedicated to the supervisors in banks throughout
the country who manage the first levels of employees—the
tellers, the bookkeepers, the checkfile clerks, the proof operators, the new accounts and customer-service personnel, the typists, and other bank personnel in clerical positions. These supervisors are the unsung heroes of banking. They are the managers in a bank who deal with minute-to-minute management problems. They have to communicate with, train, and
motivate employees who are often new to banking, and just as
often new to the experience of working for a living. The responsibilities of these first-line managers are very great because
the employees they manage provide the bank's customers with
the majority of the bank's services. If these services are not offered to customers properly, the bank will suffer financially, the
jobs of all employees in the bank will be jeopardized, and the
community that the bank serves will suffer the lack of a strong
financial institution.

The purpose of this book is to acquaint the first-line bank
supervisor with the basic concepts of management through a
practical, commonsense approach. Only experience-tested
principles of management are described. And *The Effective Bank
Supervisor* is written exclusively for bankers with their day-to-
day management problems in mind.

The first and most important principle of management is
that a manager is a manager of people. Therefore, this book

emphasizes the management of people and, of course, the manager's relationship with people. A natural corollary of this principle is that the most effective way to manage people collectively is to manage them individually. This concept will become more evident and will be developed in the chapters that follow.

Occasionally, when unavoidable, the pronoun "he" is used in reference to the manager. This pronoun is used for convenience only and is not meant to imply that most managers are men. In fact, in the past decade women have become a major source of management talent in banks. Women managers are becoming as numerous as men in the banking industry and' in the years ahead they may come to dominate management positions in banks.

The Effective Bank Supervisor covers the basic principles and skills of management in the first seven chapters. The first chapter defines the role of a manager and presents the key characteristics of a successful manager. Succeeding chapters cover the basic management functions: communicating; organizing, delegating, planning, staffing, and scheduling; decision making; training and developing employees; and motivating people. The seventh chapter is devoted to a particularly useful but often overlooked management tool—the use of statistics in bank management. And chapter eight discusses ways a manager can become more effective in developing his or her own banking career.

The Effective
Bank Supervisor

I
Introduction to Management

Definition of Management

To manage is to supervise, oversee, and direct. The management team of a bank, in a strict sense, is comprised of those employees who manage the activities of other people. This includes the president who manages the activities of the divisional vice-presidents who, in turn, manage the activities of the various departmental managers who, in turn, manage the activities of the employees in each department.

Although the principles of management are the same for all levels of managers, the techniques of applying these principles change as one climbs the management ladder. *The Effective Bank Supervisor* presents these principles as they should be understood by those who supervise the nonmanagement employees of the bank. And, because the bank department supervisor is, by definition, a manager, in this book he will most often be referred to as the manager.

A supervisor, or manager, is one who directs the activities of his department as they are performed by other people. There is a twofold assumption in this definition—that the activities of the department are directed to the best advantage of the bank and its customers, and that the employees are directed in their activities so as to produce in each the highest degree of achievement possible.

The manager's primary function is to direct the activities of other people, and so his position is unlike any other in his department. The other employees are engaged in departmental activities—operating proof machines, filing checks, waiting on customers, answering phones, etc. The manager, however, is directing these employees in the proper performance of their duties. In order to perform his job well, therefore, the manager has to become an expert in communicating with his employees, in organizing their efforts, in training them, and in motivating them to perform their duties consistently to the best of their abilities.

Characteristics of Successful Managers

There are probably scores of traits that could be listed, but the key characteristics listed here are always found to a high degree in the successful manager. These characteristics are considered to be of equal importance, and so there is no significance to the order in which they are presented.

Maturity

Maturity is that final state in a person's emotional development that permits him to understand himself and his relationships with other people. Managers who are mature are emotionally stable; they are rarely seriously shaken by unpleasant events. They are confident in their role as manager; they are not intimidated by others around them. They seldom suffer from hurt feelings; they can receive and respond to constructive criticism. They are not highly self-centered. They will admit their mistakes and not blame others for them. They are rarely prejudiced against any class of people.

Age is not an important factor in maturity. People attain full emotional maturity anytime from their early twenties to their early thirties. Some people never fully mature, but instead retain varying degrees of immaturity all their lives. Because managers interact so much with other people, they should be well on the way to full maturity before accepting managerial responsibility.

An important management skill is the ability to make sound and timely decisions. Most of the decisions a supervisor makes, directly or indirectly, affect the working lives of his department's employees. The immature supervisor will often shy away from the decision-making process entirely, and, if forced to make a decision, he will be highly influenced by the superficial and emotional opinions of others—all of which can weaken his decision to a point of almost total ineffectiveness. This weakness in the decision-making process will produce, in time, frustrations among the employees being managed. This, in turn, leads to uncooperative attitudes, poor morale, and lack of motivation. The immature supervisor, curiously, cannot understand that these negative employee reactions are a product of his own immature actions.

Empathy

Empathy is the ability to see situations as they are seen by other people—to understand other peoples' points of view and how they were formed. Empathy presupposes a genuine interest in other people—their different personalities, their likes and dislikes, their life-styles, and their behavior. Managers who are empathetic can actually project themselves into another person's personality. They are able to identify with that person's intelligence, knowledge, and social background in order to understand his reactions to real situations.

The ability to empathize can permit the manager to predict a person's reactions to potential situations too. For example, four weeks ago you hired a young and sensitive teller trainee. You trained her and put her on her own window. This afternoon she had her first difference—a twenty-five dollar shortage. She is obviously upset over the incident. You, as a manager, feel an obligation to speak to her about the shortage in order to reduce the possibility of further differences and to maintain general discipline regarding differences within the tellers' line. To be empathetic in this situation you must be able to predict

6 The Effective Bank Supervisor

the teller's reaction to varying courses of action on your part. This will require that you project yourself into the situation as if the incident had just happened to you. By recalling similar situations involving yourself and others, you should be able to relate to the natural state of worry of a sensitive person in a situation like this. The teller is worrying about losing her job. She is worrying about failing in a new job. She is worrying about what you, the manager, will do. Any strong action on your part, consequently, will only compound her worries and precipitate more differences in the days to come. Having determined through empathy the sensitivity of the situation, you decide merely to caution the teller at the proper time to be more careful in the future and not to worry about the past. The best time to do this would be just before the teller goes home, thus allowing sufficient time for the difference to be found. The conversation should be short and sympathetic.

An empathetic manager will always display fairness toward his employees; it is a vital characteristic of a good manager. People of all ages are keenly aware of those managers who are unfair with them. Employees expect fairness and will not compliment you for it. Conversely, they will react violently to unfairness and will condemn you for it. A manager cannot be fair without being empathetic.

Empathy also develops the virtue of patience, and patience is a particularly important characteristic for first-level managers to possess. Banks often hire young and inexperienced help for their clerical openings, especially in the bookkeeping, checkfile, proof, and teller areas. These employees are not only untrained in the banking business, but often they have not had a full time job before. They are not conditioned to the discipline of working within a framework of rules which is stricter than the one they may have known in a school environment. Training and supervising these employees, therefore, requires a lot of patience.

Finally, the most effective way to manage people is to manage them individually; and empathy causes the manager to relate to each employee as situations occur.

Consistent, Positive Behavior

Managers, being leaders, must be both consistent and positive in their behavior towards others. Employees look for stability in the person who directs them almost half of each waking day. People need stability in leadership just as they need stability in all aspects of their daily lives. They will become disoriented and lack confidence in a manager who vacillates between serenity and anger, fairness and unfairness, relaxation and tension, confidence and timidity, patience and impatience.

Managers can influence others, positively or negatively, with their own actions and attitudes. A manager, for example, who displays impatience, unhappiness, tension, and dissatisfaction will transmit these undesirable traits to his employees. Conversely, the positive counterparts of these traits—patience, happiness, serenity and enthusiasm—are equally contagious. If displayed consistently, they are a guiding, positive influence upon the employees. Positivism builds; negativism destroys. And seemingly neutral attitudes, because they do not promote growth, are actually a slowly destructive influence.

Propensity for Knowledge

Men are four:
He who knows not and knows
 not he knows not, he is a fool—
 shun him;
He who knows not and knows
 he knows not, he is simple—
 teach him;
He who knows and knows
 not he knows, he is asleep—
 wake him;
He who knows and knows
 he knows, he is wise—
 follow him!

Arabic Apothegm

Propensity for knowledge means not only an inclination on a manager's part to obtain knowledge, but it also implies the actual attainment of knowledge in its many forms. There is an inner circle of knowledge that a manager must have about his own department. This is followed by wider circles of knowledge, including knowing about other departments in the bank, the banking business in general, and that vast circle of knowledge about other subjects that, although apparently foreign to management, helps to develop the whole man.

A manager must know his department well. Each function of each job, and how each job relates to the other jobs in the department and to the function of the department as a whole, must be known. The best way to learn every job in the department is to do each one long enough to understand it fully. Doing the job to become proficient in it mechanically is unimportant. In managing a proof department, for example, the supervisor's goal in learning the proof operator's job is not to become the fastest operator, but rather to understand how a proof machine can be used to produce the fastest, most accurate results. He needs to know how to avoid errors in operating the machine and, of course, the best way to train a proof operator. It is a mistake for a first-line manager to think he does not have to know the details of the jobs performed by his employees. He cannot know the whole of his department without knowing each of its parts.

Knowing the relationship between his department and other departments in his division is the next circle of knowledge required for a supervisor. No department is an island unto itself. Each department receives work from other departments and sends work to other departments. The proof department, for example, receives most of its work from the teller department. After processing, "not on us" checks are sent to correspondent banks for clearance. Deposit slips and "on us" checks are sent to the bookkeeping department (or the computer center) for posting to customers' accounts. Knowledge of how the tellers process deposits, withdrawals, cashed checks and cash transactions, of how checks are cleared through the banking system, and of how the bookkeeping department and the computer center operate will be of great help to the supervisor of the proof department. The supervisor will be able to resolve dollar amount discrepancies between these departments rapidly, and will be able to devise systems to process proof work more efficiently. This will lead to lower salary costs for operating the department and less daily frustration for the employees and the manager. Aside from the day-to-day advantages of knowing the operations of these related departments, the supervisor gains a personal advantage. Because of this acquired knowledge, he may be considered for a promotion to the simultaneous management of two or more of these departments.

The supervisor's knowledge, however, should not be confined to his department and division alone. A knowledge of all facets of banking is essential in the development of the well-informed banker, and so the supervisor should become familiar with the functions of all the divisions within the bank. The more he knows about all aspects of banking, the better he will be in performing his own job and in preparing himself for future responsibilities.

We live in a rapidly changing world. During the past 25 years there have been more changes in banking in this country than there have been during its whole 200 year history. Consider the changes in banking that have taken place due to electronics alone. Computer technology has produced new banking services, faster ways of handling paper documents, and more comprehensive reports. Automation has led to a new banking terminology that includes such words and phrases as MICR (Magnetic Ink Character Recognition), CRT (Cathode Ray Tube), CIF (Central Information File), online teller terminal, automated clearing house, electronic proof machines, microfiche records, and continuous compounding of interest. New techniques, new products, and new markets for banking services are being developed each year. Progress and growth are a product of change. To be fully effective in their roles, managers must be informed of these changes; they can accomplish this by reading banking periodicals, conversing with other bankers, and attending professional seminars.

Any discussion about knowledge should include a few comments on education. Education is the attainment of knowledge that raises us to a higher level of thought about ourselves and our relationships with others. Specifically, it includes the study of history, literature, religion, philosophy, languages, music, art, the social sciences, and the physical sciences. Education can remove the chains from our minds and allow us to understand better, appreciate more, and have greater compassion for others—their life-styles and their points of view. Education, therefore, promotes empathy.

Knowledge itself, and the process of acquiring knowledge in all subjects, informs us of facts and ideas. More importantly, however, it teaches us to refine our process of judgment, to think, to reason, to investigate, to analyze, to compare, and to sharpen our imagination. And all these activities are important tools of management.

Finally, through knowledge comes wisdom. Wisdom is the application of knowledge to everyday living and working situations. Knowledge in itself is relatively useless to a person unless it is constantly applied both to present situations and potential ones.

The wise man knows that there can be knowledge without wisdom, but not wisdom without knowledge.

Ability to Make Decisions

Decision making is developing the correct course of action for the solution of a problem. If there were only one factor that differentiated a manager from the workers, it would certainly be the necessity for managers to make decisions. Employees rely on managers to make decisions. Managers rely on themselves to make decisions. Each working day, a barrage of problems requiring decisions is presented to the bank manager. These decisions can be personnel-related, involving staffing, scheduling, time-off, salary, performance appraisals, discipline, counseling, training and motivating. They can be work related, involving equipment needs, work-flows and methods, expense approvals, check and withdrawal approvals, customer problems, etc. Decision making is so vital that, without the ability and willingness to make decisions, a manager cannot manage at all. The subject of decision making is presented in more detail later in this book.

Spirit of Accomplishment

When the senior management of a bank looks among the ranks of first-level managers for those capable of being promoted, a prominent factor in their evaluation is the manager's ability to accomplish those things that are beyond the ordinary.

Managers who accomplish the extraordinary take their managerial duties beyond the routine by constantly looking for ways to improve their departments. Through thought, imagination, research and experimentation, they develop ways of decreasing expenses, increasing income, providing better customer service, and providing better employee training. They are pathfinders, not pathfollowers. They anticipate potential problems and so are equipped to cope with or avoid these problems. They do not wait for their superiors to spur them into action. They move ahead independently and implement proper courses of action. They don't just talk about changes; they make changes. They are challenged by new and different assignments. They enjoy success with quiet pride. These managers are motivated by accomplishment. They have what every manager must work to develop—a spirit of accomplishment!

II
Communicating

Humans have the unique ability to communicate with each other by means of language. In prehistoric times only the spoken word was used. Early forms of writing consisted of picture writing, as evidenced by the drawings found on the walls of early man's cave dwellings. These pictures depicted events, but could convey only general meanings. They had no fixed connection to the spoken word. More advanced picture-writing techniques, such as the ancient Egyptian hieroglyphic system, used pictures of objects to represent not only the objects themselves, but also alphabetic sounds and often complete syllables of the spoken word. Full alphabetic writing of a language was first developed by the ancient Greek civilization in about 800 B.C. From this Greek alphabet the Roman civilization developed its Latin alphabet. The English alphabet we use today is a slightly modified version of the Roman-Latin alphabet.

The development of the alphabet was the most important communications achievement of mankind. It provided man with a means to convert his spoken language to a uniform written language. This permitted him to communicate with other people in distant places. The written language, moreover, preserved for future generations man's knowledge, thoughts, and accomplishments.

Communication in Management

Managers organize, train, and motivate other people in the performance of their duties. In order to perform these functions a manager must be able to convey his thoughts to others and he also must let others convey their thoughts to him. This alternating flow of thoughts between manager and employee is communication—the basic tool of management.

Throughout this chapter references are made to the three essential parts of a communication—the sender, the message, and the receiver. The sender is the person who communicates the message; the message is what is being communicated; and the receiver is the person to whom the message is being communicated. There can be no communication if any of these parts is missing.

Sender + Message + Receiver = Communication

Oral Communication

The primary means of communicating with other people is through the use of language—both in spoken and written form. For a supervisor, however, the use of the spoken word predominates over all other forms of communication. It is used in all the day-to-day directing of employees—answering and asking questions, coordinating work efforts, instructing, correcting, appraising, counseling, etc. Basically, there are only two ways of communicating orally with others—person-to-person or in a group. The most widely used and generally most effective way for a manager to communicate is on an individual basis. This is the purest form of communication. It permits the free flow of ideas and thoughts between only two people. It eliminates the possibly distracting thoughts or unwanted influences of others. Personnel-related topics such as an employee's salary, absenteeism, and job performance should always be discussed on an individual basis.

Communicating to employees on a group basis should be limited to those occasions when the primary function of the meeting is to inform employees of items of general interest—e.g. new bank services, new bank facilities, reorganization of the department, changes in the physical appearance of the department, new equipment about to be delivered, promotions, transfers, and the like. Training employees in the use of new equipment or instructing them in new operating procedures can be done successfully in a group. New procedures, however, should be first communicated in writing before being explained at a meeting. (These and other training techniques will be fully discussed in chapter 5, "Training and Developing Employees.")

Some supervisors attempt in a departmental meeting to solve problems related to the bad habits of some of the employees in the department. According to their theory, a speech by the supervisor on tardiness, for example, will be absorbed by those who are tardy. But this approach is ineffective in solving the problem. Critical remarks made in a meeting are usually absorbed by no one. The offenders invariably think that the supervisor is referring to someone else. Parenthetically, complimentary remarks are accepted by everyone—deserving or not. The most effective way to solve any problem related to poor personal habits (tardiness, absenteeism, sloppiness, etc.) is to talk to each offender individually.

Supervisors are often disappointed in a group meeting when there is no feedback or exchange of ideas. Assuming that the supervisor is not too dominant and that he does not use the meeting as a forum exclusively for his thoughts, the problem is not with the manager but rather with the employees. In the type of group communication discussed so far, the group consists of ten or fifteen employees of different backgrounds, interests, and personalities assembled for a meeting. Therefore, these meetings should be held for informational purposes only. The employees will listen to what is being said at these meetings, but the supervisor should not expect creativity, a constant flow of questions, and a high degree of involvement from such a mixed group of clerical employees. Many employees do not actively participate in meetings for a variety of reasons—too shy, afraid of saying the wrong thing, intimidated by other senior employees, not interested in or familiar with the subject, etc. Successful creative meetings can be conducted with clerical employees, however, if the meetings are well planned and properly conducted. Specific guidelines for a meeting of this type are presented later in this chapter.

Written Communication

Although most communications made by a first-line bank manager are oral, the use of the written language is required, if not preferred on many occasions. There are three types of written communications—narrative, graphic, and statistical. Narrative writing is used in reports to higher management, job descriptions, job procedures, memorandums, and letter writing. Graphics, which involves the use of charts, diagrams, graphs, and drawings, is a form of written communication which is particularly useful in training employees. Statistics is the scientific use of numbers for reporting and comparing. Statistical writing is often combined with charts and graphs to illustrate dramatically the major points in a report. Examples of graphic and statistical writing, and a fuller discussion of these subjects, are presented in the chapters on training and the use of statistics (chapters 5 and 7).

Converting one's ideas into narrative writing requires thought, time, and a working knowledge of the English language. Even though most managers do not have much opportunity to communicate in writing, they should practice the art of writing whenever possible. Writing is the best way to organize ideas and thoughts. It is an excellent way to learn the use of the language, and that in turn can dramatically improve one's speaking ability. Volumes have been written on how to write. But one small book outlines succinctly the basic concepts of narrative writing. It is *Elements of Style* by William Strunk, Jr., and E. B. White, published by The MacMillan Company.

Advantages and Disadvantages

There are three main advantages to communicating orally rather than in writing. It is faster; it provides an opportunity for immediate feedback; and it gives both parties involved the opportunity to express themselves through gestures as well as words. Short messages, assuming both parties are physically in the same location, are always faster to convey orally than in writing. For instance, if the manager wished to tell the parking lot attendant to put an overdue parking notice on the new red sports car that has been parked all morning in the bank's customer parking lot, the manager would merely mention it to the attendant. There would be no need to take the time to write a memorandum. To point out the importance of feedback in this example, the attendant would have the immediate opportunity to tell the manager that the new red sports car belongs to the president of the bank!

Feedback is an important advantage of oral communications; because the parties involved in the communication are physically present, the opportunity to determine whether the message was received and understood is always present. In written communications, however, the writer is never immediately positive that the message was even received, or read, or understood. The subject of feedback in oral communications is treated more fully later in this chapter.

Oral person-to-person communications also provide an opportunity for the parties involved to express themselves physically. As will be discussed in the next section of this chapter, the use of the voice, facial expressions, and gestures provides both the sender and the receiver with a wide range of ways to accent and dramatize their thoughts. Physical expression is a major advantage of oral communications because it so often increases the effectiveness of the message.

Written communications have several advantages. The human mind is far more capable of learning and remembering a highly detailed message that is seen (read from prose or viewed through graphics) rather than one that is heard. Job descriptions, complicated operating procedures, personnel policies and the like, therefore, should always be written. Writing a communication also gives the sender an opportunity to present a well-thought-out logical message. In oral communications the danger of communicating a disorganized or perhaps unintentionally insulting message is always present. Once an ill-advised oral message is communicated, it cannot be erased. Another major advantage of written communications is that they are documented for future reference. The written word is permanent history. File cabinets and libraries are filled with people's written communications to other people, whereas the spoken word is a fleeting event, soon forgotten and lost forever. Finally, in the business environment, some messages, regardless of length, should be in writing to add formality and an official note to the communication. A notice to employees regarding a new, upcoming bank holiday, for example, should be in writing. Even though it may be brief, the notice is official, not rumor, because it is in writing.

The disadvantages of both oral and written communications logically stem from the advantages of each. For example, since an advantage of the oral communication is that it provides an opportunity for immediate feedback, then a disadvantage of written communication is that it does not provide an opportunity for immediate feedback. Since an advantage of a written communication is that it is documented for future reference, then a disadvantage of an oral communication is that it is not documented for future reference. Figure 1 includes a list of the disadvantages of both types of communications.

Physical Communication

The human body offers a powerful and often profound means of expression. Through the use of the voice, facial expressions, and body signs and movements, a person can communicate emotions, emphasize his meaning, and show interest in other people. The voice can communicate joy or amusement

Figure 1

Oral and Written Communications Summary Chart

	Oral	Written
Types:	Individual Group	Narrative Graphic Statistical

When used:	Asking questions
	Answering questions
	Giving directions
	Coordinating work efforts
	Appraising
	Counseling
	Instructing
	Conducting employee
	    meetings
	Making general announce-
	    ments
		Official announcements
		Reports to management
		Job descriptions
		Job procedures
		Operating Procedures
		Memorandums
		Letters
		Training aids
		Events requiring documen-
		    tation

Advantages:	Fast
	Immediate feedback
	Physical communications
	    possible
		Can be highly detailed
		Documented for future
		    reference
		Often better composed
		More formal and official
		Easier to remember

Disadvantages:	Cannot be highly detailed
	Not documented for
	    reference
	Often poorly composed
	More difficult to
	    remember
	Less formal and official
		Slow
		No immediate feedback
		Physical communications
		    not possible

in laughing, sorrow in crying, anger in yelling, pleasure in singing, secrecy in whispering, and displeasure in growling or muttering. Voice inflections can accent words or phrases, present a question, or deliver an exclamation.

The variety of facial expressions available for communicating are almost legion. Consider the inquisitive look, the mischievous glance, the bored yawn, the astonished gape, the disbelieving smirk, and the suspicious frown. The most powerful of all physical expressions, however, is the smile. The smile is so effective because it communicates positive attitudes and emotions towards other people. The smile can express joy, pleasure, understanding, approval, love, and friendship. The smile of a manager can communicate to a new employee acceptance into the group and the impression that the manager is happy that the employee is in the department. A manager's smile expresses to an older employee the mutual loyalty and friendship that has existed through the years. The smile recognizes the importance of the individual and it is a key physical communicator for the manager.

All facial expressions involve the use of the eyes. Looking at someone while communicating is for most people a natural thing to do. Its importance, however, cannot be emphasized too strongly. The eyes are the most important part of the facial expression. They must be seen by both the sender and the receiver so that the full impact of the communication can be received.

Finally, many body signs and movements can be used to communicate. Some of these are the hello and goodbye wave, beckoning and pointing signs, the handshake, sizing (using the hands to denote the size of an object), and counting (using fingers to show the number of objects). Even posture can communicate—the erect body denotes formality and seriousness, and the relaxed body denotes informality and openness.

An experienced interviewer of job applicants knows that the best way to get an applicant to talk is to make him feel relaxed. And in order to communicate a relaxed atmosphere, the interviewer must look relaxed himself. The simple physical act of assuming a relaxed position in his chair, perhaps leaning back with hands folded in front of him or resting on the arms of his chair, will automatically convey a relaxed atmosphere. The results of these simple physical communications are often remarkable. Applicants will almost always, as if responding to an invisible signal, relax in their chairs. This technique is equally effective in any situation where the manager wishes to relax an employee who may be apprehensive.

Although physical expressions can be used by themselves in communicating, more often they are used as a dramatic complement to person-to-person oral communications. The following simple example shows the advantages of augmenting oral communications with physical.

It is 6:30 P.M. in the bookkeeping department. All the employees have apparently gone home. The manager, Arline Johnson, is sitting at her desk at one end of the half-darkened room, working intently on a report to be presented the following morning.

Suddenly the silence is interrupted by a faint but audible voice way at the other end of the room by the exit door saying, "Good night." Arline instantly recognizes the voice of Jane Carpenter, a recently hired checkfile clerk. At this point Arline has several options:

1. Pretending she didn't hear the faint voice—no communication.
2. Saying in a monotone voice without looking up, "Good night"—oral communication only.
3. Waving good-bye without looking up—body sign only.
4. Looking up, smiling, and waving—facial expression and body sign.
5. Looking up, smiling, waving, and saying in a warm voice but loud enough to be heard, "Good night, Jane, see you tomorrow"—facial expression, body sign, and voice expression combined with oral communication.

Obviously, the most effective choice would be number five. It combines all of the physical forms of communication (voice, facial expression and body movement) with oral communication. The mere words "good night" could have been used, but much more was added with the physical complements of the smile, the warm voice, and the wave.

The lesson to be learned in communicating with other people is that the more types of communication used in combination, the more effective and personal the communication becomes. The manager is a manager of people. In the example just described, there is no doubt that by using alternative number five, the new employee, Jane, would go home that night with a positive impression of being liked and accepted in her new position. This example is of a minor incident in the daily work routine; but by consistently choosing the fifth alternative in all communication efforts, the manager will build a rapport and a sense of caring, and he will communicate his messages more effectively.

Alternative number one in the above example introduces a subject that is an adjunct to physical communications—no communication at all. A manager is communicating even when he is not communicating. Had Arline ignored the incident, Jane would have received a message: that the manager was too busy to be bothered by her and that she was not important enough to interrupt the manager. If the president of the bank had said "Good night," the manager would have communicated! Managers cannot afford negative communications such as this. They rely on the employees in the department to do the work. They must not pass up any opportunity to communicate and to recognize the individual whenever and wherever possible. If an occasion arises where several employees are involved, then all of them have to be recognized equally. No one should be left out.

Finally, there is a form of physical communication that is seldom recognized as a means of communicating—communicating by example. Managers, whether intentionally or not, are continually communicating to their employees by their example. Managers must practice what they preach. If, for example, they wish their employees to be precise and accurate in their work, then they must show these qualities in their own work. Employees expect more from their managers than they do from their co-workers or even from themselves. They expect managers to be knowledgeable, understanding, accurate, and patient, and they will watch for these and other positive traits. Managers set the pattern of what is expected from the employees; they are always subtly teaching by example. And they are always communicating by example, whether by doing something positive, something negative, or even by not doing anything at all.

In conclusion, physical communication, though it can be used successfully alone, is primarily used to accent, to dramatize and to add warmth to oral communication. Some supervisors may find it difficult to express themselves physically. Fortunately, physical communication is an art that can be learned easily by closely observing and practicing the desirable voice inflections, facial expressions, and body movements of others. The use of a mirror will be helpful in practicing facial expressions, and a tape recorder will help in isolating and replacing unwanted voice inflections with desirable ones. Above all, the supervisor has to learn to use often the one physical expression that will always communicate positive feelings—the smile.

Techniques in Oral Communication

Since first-line bank managers spend the majority of their time communicating orally, they should know how to relate their ideas and thoughts to others effectively. What follows is a discussion of several techniques that should, through practice, become an integral part of every important communication. Although the techniques described refer to oral communications, many of them are of equal importance in preparing a written communication.

Organizing the Communication

> If your lips would keep
>   from slips,
> Five things observe with care:
> To whom you speak, of whom you speak,
> and how and when and where.
>   William Edward Norris

A communication should be organized. There are five steps involved. These are to decide what, to whom, how, when, and where to communicate.

Decide what is to be communicated. The supervisor should define the subject matter in his mind. If it is complicated, it should be written down for reference so that important points won't be forgotten during the communication. The possible repercussions, implications or misrepresentations that might occur should be researched in order to prepare a proper explanation. Take, for example, Bob Thompson, the bank's messenger, whose salary review is due. During the last few weeks you've noticed a marked change in Bob's attitude on the job for no apparent reason. You have, therefore, decided to defer recommending a salary increase until Bob's attitude is reversed. A possible repercussion of communicating this to Bob is that, if the communication is not handled properly, he will become discouraged and his attitude will become even worse. Bob might also suspect that it may be a long time before his salary is reviewed again. So the interview should be designed with these possibilities taken into consideration. A sample outline of what should be said during the interview follows:

1. State that the salary review is due.
2. State that you have noticed a marked change in attitude.
3. Ask Bob the reason for the attitude change.
4. If no reasons are given, prompt him. "A problem with some employee in the department? Problem at home? Possibly a problem with me (you, his manager)?" This is always the last prompting question asked.
5. Upon finding out the reasons, counsel him to improve. Note: Steps 1, 2, 3, and 4 will reduce the risk that Bob will be discouraged by demonstrating that you, the manager, want to help.
6. Explain that you seriously hesitate to recommend a salary increase until his attitude changes for the better, but that perhaps a month or at most six weeks would be long enough for you to wait to review the situation again.
7. Promise to discuss the situation again with Bob whenever he may wish but no longer than six weeks from today.

Note: Steps 6 and 7 avoid the possibility that Bob will infer that it may be a long time before his salary is reviewed again.

Decide to whom to communicate. In most communication situations, it is obvious to whom the message is to be directed. If there is more than one person who is to receive the same message, however, it may not be obvious whether the message is better communicated individually or in a group. In almost all personnel-related situations (those involving appraising, correcting, salary review, time off, motivating, counseling, etc.), the message should be communicated to each person individually. This preserves confidentiality and will allow proper feedback. Even if there are a number of employees who have an absenteeism problem, for example, each employee should be counseled separately. Do not try to save time or reduce the unpleasantness of the situation by talking to everyone involved at the same time. It will be ineffective. As was mentioned before and will be mentioned again, the best way to manage people collectively is to manage them individually. In some situations, communicating the same message to several employees at once can be very effective. These are situations involving the orientation and training of new employees, the dissemination of messages of general interest, and the answering of factual questions.

Communicating a message through another party should be avoided unless the message is both extremely simple and nonpersonal. It is difficult enough to communicate something correctly to a person directly without relying on the comprehension and memory powers of another party. Messages are never relayed by the other party exactly in the same manner as they were intended by the original sender. As the saying goes, something was lost in the translation. Often the whole intent of the message is lost.

Finally, some situations require interviewing a number of employees about the same problem. Since problem situations require talking to each employee individually, the supervisor should consciously decide in what order each is to be interviewed. If, for example, a group of employees in the proof department is complaining indirectly, through others, about working late hours, then a good solution would be to poll each employee in the section. As a general rule, the employees should be interviewed according to the status of their position, starting with the employee of highest status. Often in situations like this, all employees have the same position and, therefore, the polling order is determined by seniority, starting with the employee with the most seniority. This approach has three advantages: it recognizes the status of each employee in the group; it may determine in the supervisor's mind whether the older employees are influencing the younger employees; and the supervisor may be able to determine whether certain job groups or seniority groups are more affected by the situation than others.

Decide how, when, and where to communicate. Depending on whether the message is instructive, corrective or informative, the method of communicating should be decided on in advance. Instructive and informative communications, such as answering questions, giving directions, training, orienting, and relating interesting news of general interest, require a more relaxed, conversational atmosphere with consideration given to the use of graphics and statistics. Corrective situations, such as those involving personnel problems, should be handled in a more formal and serious atmosphere. The kind of physical communication used to augment the oral communication will greatly help to establish and maintain the correct atmosphere.

Closely related to the way of communicating is the when and where of the communication. All serious corrective situations require a place that is private in order to establish the correct atmosphere, to avoid interruptions, and to eliminate the possibility of someone overhearing the conversation. Training and orientation sessions also require privacy principally to avoid interruptions. Privacy, however, is often difficult to find in a busy bank department. The time of communication is often determined by the availability of a private place. Timing is discussed more fully with regard to correcting and training employees in the chapter on training (chapter 5).

Presenting the Subject

The following techniques should be used during any oral communication initiated by a manager.

Introduce the subject. Even though the manager knows well what he plans to talk about, he should not assume that the employee knows. Many employees, if the communication is at all formal, are apprehensive about being called to a manager's desk or office. They generally think that the conversation will be about something they did wrong. If this is not the situation, this should be mentioned first to put the employee's mind at ease so that he will be receptive to the message. A remark such as "Don't worry, there is nothing wrong" followed by an introduction to the subject such as "I would like to talk to you about your vacation schedule," or "It's time to talk about your salary review," will both eliminate the apprehension and introduce the subject at the same time.

If in fact the subject is about something that requires criticism, then this subject should also be introduced at the beginning of the conversation. It is important to be direct and to the point. This will decrease the employee's natural apprehension. What is important to remember about introducing any subject is never to assume that the employee knows the topic of the communication, and always to introduce the subject at the beginning of the conversation.

Choose the correct words. The purpose of a communication is to transmit a message to someone else. The manager has to use words, therefore, that an employee can understand. If, for example, you are talking to a teller about his loquacious manner with customers, the teller, not knowing the definition of the word "loquacious," may think you are complimenting him rather than counseling him about being too talkative. Managers should use simple universally understood words. Messages should be communicated in short sentences. Long and complicated sentences are much more difficult to understand in speaking than in writing. Written sentences can be reviewed again by the reader. Since the spoken sentence is presented only once, it is either misunderstood or not understood at all if it is too complicated.

More specifically, however, managers often tend to use technical banking terms in their speech with employees because these terms are so commonly used in the manager's communications with peers or higher management. These terms are a part of a manager's daily vocabulary. They are not, however, necessarily part of an employee's vocabulary. This is particularly true of new employees who have never heard the hundreds of banking terms that are used daily. Seemingly simple messages like "Please bring me the proof tapes that are on the Recordak machine" or "Ask the customer for an updated corporate resolution" might not even be understood by a new employee. The words "proof tapes," "Recordak," and "corporate resolution" are banking terms and may not yet be part of a new employee's vocabulary. Even older employees are often unfamiliar with banking terms that are used in other departments. Managers should choose words that employees, depending on their educational and work background, will understand, or they should define those words that could be misunderstood.

Common and sometimes amusing situations, which show the need for defining a word, often occur in the use of employees' first names. A manager, for example, tells an employee to tell another employee that her husband is on the phone. He says "Tell Nancy that her husband is on the phone." The employee dutifully goes to Nancy and gives her the message. Nancy picks up the phone and says "Hi, Honey!" Immediately she realizes it is not her husband on the phone. The problem was that there were two married employees named Nancy in the department, and the employee delivering the message for the manager went to the nearest Nancy who, of course, was the wrong one. Experienced managers can relate many stories, both amusing and otherwise, concerning mixups over using employees' first names only. In such circumstances, it is best to use both the first and last name.

Managers should not use any words that ridicule or otherwise attack an employee's ego or self-esteem. Comments like "I know you usually have trouble learning new things, but..." or "Even though you have a light educational background, perhaps..." should be avoided. The employee immediately will focus on the critical remark and will have been distracted from receiving the remainder of the message. Only the critical remark will have been received and remembered.

Of the millions of words in the English language the word "I" and a person's name rank highest in popularity. Managers, however, are best advised not to use the word "I" when giving directions ("I want you to do..." and "I would like you to..." etc.). The use of the word "I" in this instance, because of the many directions given to employees during the day, gives the consistent impression that the manager is forcing his will upon them. Beginning the direction with language like "Would you please...?" or "Will you...?" or "Please..." is much more acceptable and equally effective.

The use of the employee's name should be used generously during any communication. The name identifies the individual specifically. When used by the manager, a name personalizes the conversation. Even if the communication is merely a "Good morning!" it is much more personal to say "Good morning, Jenny."

Using Special Speech Techniques

Since the time of the ancient Greek and Roman cultures, people have developed ways of speaking that create interest, keep the listener's attention, drive home important points, dramatize, emphasize, and persuade. These techniques comprise the art of rhetoric. Rhetoric is a principle course of study required for those engaging in oratory and/or public speaking. Although managers need not be public speakers nor engage in oratory, they must effectively communicate with others. What follows, therefore, is a discussion of some rhetorical techniques which can be easily used in many of the manager's day-to-day communications.

Hyperbole, anecdotes, quotations, and humor. These are techniques that can be easily introduced into most communications. An hyperbole is an exaggerated statement. Phrases like "Those records are stacked a mile high," "That experience is worth a million dollars," and "It will take forever to file those checks" are hyperboles. Hyperboles are used to dramatize a point.

An anecdote is a personal, interesting story that is related to the subject being communicated. Anecdotes attract and retain interest and dramatize points to be made.

Quotations are used to call upon a higher authority on the subject being presented. If the authority is well-known and recognized, the quotation can be very effective in persuading the listener to accept the point being made. Formal remarks made by the chairman of the board or by the president of your bank, or from well-written articles in banking publications are typically good sources.

The introduction of humor in a long serious conversation is often a welcome pause for both parties. In the manager-employee communication, humor is not joke telling, but rather remarks of a lighthearted nature. Too much serious conversation can overburden both parties. Humor, used in good taste and at the right moment, will relieve the burden of seriousness just long enough to refresh both parties before the conversation is continued. Like all the techniques described in this section, however, it should be used for accent in communication and not for its own sake.

Triplets, anaphora, and alliteration. The use of triplets and the repetition of words and sounds in anaphora and alliteration are unfortunately seldom used by managers. These three forms of language expression, with only a little forethought required, can be very powerful speech techniques for the manager, particularly in his role as trainer and counselor.

Triplets are the presentation of thoughts about a subject in a group of three words or phrases. Alliteration is the repetition in close succession of the same sound, usually the same first letter in succeeding words. Anaphora is the repetition of the same word or phrase at the beginning of successive phrases, clauses, or sentences. Alliteration and anaphora are often combined with triplets for a more dramatic effect.

The written and spoken words of famous people throughout the centures illustrate the power of these techniques: "I came. I saw. I conquered." combines anaphora with triplets; "Friends, Romans, countrymen, lend me your ears" utilizes triplets; "... Life, Liberty and the pursuit of Happiness" combines alliteration with triplets; and "...we can not dedicate, we can not consecrate, we can not hallow this ground" combines anaphora with triplets.

To illustrate the more practical application of these techniques in a banking environment, two stories (anecdotes) can be told. An elderly senior bank officer was asked by a young married couple "What things should we look for when buying a home?" He answered, "There are three things to consider when buying a home: location, location, and location." This exemplifies the use of triplets. The second story concerns a bank personnel officer who was about to begin the training of an inexperienced interviewer of job applicants. The personnel officer, knowing that an important part of interviewing people to fill job openings is to know the type of people to look for, thought and thought of a way to reduce this complex subject to a basic principle that could be easily understood and remembered. Finally, after much thought, he told the new interviewer, "There are three things to look for in any applicant for any job opening: personality, proficiency, and permanence." This exemplifies the use of alliteration combined with triplets.

Inviting Feedback

Even though a manager may be very good at communicating a message to an employee, he never knows for certain that the message was received unless a response is invited from the employee. This response is called feedback. Feedback is always important in communicating because it helps to insure that the message was received, and received correctly. The need for feedback is often displayed in the employee's physical reactions or lack of them. Nervous mannerisms, blank stares, and the like are good indications that the message is not being received. Questioning or puzzled looks indicate that the message is being received but not fully understood.

When the employee makes a statement related to a previous remark by the manager immediately after the manager has remarked on another point, this is a tell-tale sign that at least part of the message has not been received. Between the time of the manager's remark that triggered the statement and the time the employee actually made the statement, the employee most likely did not receive any other messages. That time was being used by the employee to think about the statement that he was going to make. This problem often comes up when the communication concerns the employee personally in an area such as job performance. The following example should illustrate this more clearly.

The supervisor of the new accounts department is talking to Mike, a new accounts representative, about his apparent unwillingness to help the other employees in the department by doing his share of the miscellaneous clerical duties. The supervisor states the problem to Mike, and cites a few examples of Mike's unwillingness. He then continues to explain at length how important it is that the clerical work is done and that each person does his share. Immediately after the supervisor has finished, Mike replies that he can't understand why the supervisor feels the way he does. Mike then begins reciting a list of clerical jobs he has done during the past few weeks and how he has noticed that other employees were not doing their share. It is safe to assume that Mike did not hear the supervisor's lengthy explanation of the importance of the clerical duties because he was too busy thinking up a rebuttal to the supervisor's first critical remarks about his unwillingness.

In order to avoid this type of problem, the supervisor should have paused after introducing the subject of Mike's unwillingness to perform required clerical duties. During the pause, the supervisor should have invited Mike to comment with such questions as "Do you have anything to say about this?" or "Do you think my judgement of your unwillingness is substantially correct?" After Mike had responded, the supervisor then could recite his views on the importance of the clerical work with a higher probability of these remarks being heard.

Pauses for feedback should be introduced several times during conversations—especially after each major part of the message. During these pauses, the manager should invite the employee's comments and questions. If an adequate response is not forthcoming, the manager can prompt a response by asking direct questions.

Developing Receptiveness

"Speech is silvern, silence is golden."
Carlyle

So far in this discussion of oral communication techniques, the emphasis has been on how the manager should present messages to employees. Of equal importance is how managers should receive messages from employees. It seems to be a natural tendency in people that, when communicating, they are interested more in sending messages than in receiving them —they would rather talk than listen. Managers are no exception, but because of their position in the department they could easily dominate all communication situations. Managers, however, must know what is on the minds of their employees in order to direct them properly. They must, therefore, both allow and encourage employees to speak as much and as often as necessary. Then they must listen to what the employee is saying.

Encouraging employees to communicate. A manager cannot listen to employees if they are hesitant to speak to him. An old adage says, If the parent is listening to the child at the age of six, the child will be talking to the parent at the age of sixteen. Even though the manager-employee relationship is not the same as the parent-child relationship, there is a lesson in communicating to be learned from this adage. Encouraging employees to communicate is a continual and subtle process. If the employee says, "Good morning!" to you, do you return the greeting pleasantly? If the employee comes up to your desk and says, "Are you very busy?" do you say, "I'm never too busy for you" or "Yes, I'll see you later."? If you have an office, is your office door open most of the time or closed most of the time? If an employee happens to mention that he just bought a new car, do you say, "That's nice" and walk away, or do you say, "Won't you tell me about it?"

Managers should never be too busy to communicate with their employees. Their main function is to relate to their employees; and they can't relate to them if they close off communications with them. Employees don't distinguish between an important communication and an unimportant one. They form impressions of a manager's interest in listening to them from all communication situations, as they occur, day after day after day.

The preceding examples imply that the supervisor should be physically available to the employees. Supervisors who are out of their departments often, continually talking on the telephone, or constantly attending meetings are not available. The employee cannot talk to a supervisor who isn't available.

The story is told of a successful manager of a large manufacturing plant employing several hundred people who *each day* walked through the large, sprawling plant to greet and talk to employees. When asked why he spent so much time touring the plant so often, he responded, "I want the employees to know that I'm interested in them and in communicating with them." Very few if any bank departments are as large as this manufacturing plant. Bank managers should make it a point to talk to each of their employees each day. This will encourage employees to communicate.

Listening. Listening is an art which managers must develop. Sending messages is only one half of the communicating process; receiving messages (listening) is the other half. Almost every communication, regardless of whether it is initiated by the supervisor or the employee, involves both speaking and listening. The following points will be helpful in developing the art of listening.

1. Show willingness to listen. When the employee is speaking, appear relaxed. Focus all your attention on him. Don't allow yourself to be distracted. Although you may be burdened with a hundred other problems, when the employee speaks, you should be thinking of nothing else.
2. Show interest in what is being said. This involves being empathetic. Project yourself into the speaker's point of view. Understand not only what he is saying, but also why he is saying it. By using appropriate facial expressions and one or two word comments like "Oh," "Yes," "I understand," "Continue," and "Give me an example," the employee will know you are listening and are interested. He will be encouraged to say more.
3. Don't interrupt the employee's train of thought. Allow sufficient time for the employee to finish what he wants to say. Ask questions later when there is a natural pause. Do not introduce a foreign subject into the speaker's mind with a statement like, "I understand, but that reminds me of something else I've been meaning to ask you ..."
4. Take notes. There are many occasions that will require taking short notes while listening. These notes then can be used later in the conversation to ask clarifying questions, or, after the communication has been concluded, as an aid to remembering key points. Note-taking during a conversation can be disconcerting to the speaker, however, unless the following simple courtesies are observed:
    a. Before beginning, mention to the speaker that you might take a few notes as an aid to remembering. If this isn't done, the speaker won't know for certain what you are doing with the pencil and paper.
    b. Take very short notes consisting of key words and phrases.
    c. Do not take the notes continously during the conversation, but rather as an aid in remembering a key point.
5. Be ready to help the speaker. When talking to managers, employees often find it difficult to express themselves. Be

ready to help them when they are obviously groping for the right words or phrases.

6. Overlook apparently attacking remarks. Questions like, "Why isn't something done about the lack of cooperation in the department?" or "Why aren't newer employees being trained the way they should be?" are usually not meant to be a direct attack upon the manager, even though solving those problems are his direct responsibility. They are merely statements of fact, as observed by the speaker, and said without regard to diplomacy. Remember that employees should not be expected to be as good communicators as managers.

7. Don't be prejudiced by the speaker. There are some people to whom managers tend not to listen. Typical of these are the "talker" and the "complainer." People who talk too much or who speak in a complaining way automatically set up a negative attitude in the manager. The manager tends either to turn off the speaker, in his mind, or to immediately look for ways of removing himself from the speaker's presence. Managers, however, cannot afford not to listen to these employees because they often have worthwhile messages to convey. It is only their way of speaking that is undesirable, not necessarily their message.

8. Be aware of the speaker's eloquence and emotional impact. Frequently a manager will be communicating with employees in his department, peers, members of higher management, and customers, who are able to speak the language eloquently and/or with emotion. That is, these people are very capable of presenting their message convincingly. Such speakers are the well-spoken, lucid, irate customer, the upset, perhaps tearful employee, and the well-educated, eloquent senior officer. When listening to these and other kinds of convincing speakers, the important thing to remember is to identify and evaluate the content of the message, and not to be influenced by the method used to deliver the message. Eloquence and emo-

tion in speech do not automatically mean accuracy in content. Some of the most illogical, uninformed comments have come from the mouths of the eloquent.

9. Listen for what is not said. What is not said can often convey a message of equal or greater importance than what is said. Determining what has not been said involves a certain amount of preparation before the communication begins or reflection after the communication ends. A manager of a teller department, for example, when interviewing applicants for teller openings, would particularly want to hear that they would enjoy working with the public. When an applicant omits this or a like statement upon being asked, "What attracts you to the teller opening?" the manager should immediately recognize the omission. By predetermining the kind of answers the manager would like to hear in response to questions, the importance of what has not been said will automatically be recognized.

10. Be silent. The human mind is remarkable and highly versatile. There is one thing, however, it cannot do. It cannot send and receive a message at the same time. If a manager wants to listen, he cannot talk. The truly communicative manager will listen 80 percent of the time and speak only 20 percent of the time. Managers must learn what is going on in the minds of their employees. This learning can only be done through listening.

Listening is a function that is especially vital during interviews. In the job interview, the manager wants to learn about the applicant, his strengths, weaknesses, likes and dislikes, his personality, etc. In the counseling interview, the manager wants to learn what is troubling the employee, what is hindering his performance. The whole object of interviewing is to get the employee to speak, and then to listen intently to what the employee is saying.

To illustrate the importance of listening, a true, but edited, story can be told. This story is about a New England bank personnel officer and an exit interview that he conducted with an employee who was about to leave the bank for another job. A week before the employee, whom we shall name Beverly, was to leave, the personnel officer was tipped off by another officer in the bank that if he, the personnel officer, could get Beverly to talk in an exit interview, the interview would be very revealing about what was going on in Beverly's department. The personnel officer, having long suspected that there were problems in this department, saw at last an opportunity to determine the extent of these problems. Accordingly, he prepared for the interview with the care that a diplomat might use to prepare for a meeting with a foreign secretary of state. The preparation and execution of the interview required using many of the techniques of listening and communicating that have been described in this chapter.

Timing the interview was a critical factor. The personnel officer knew that, when conducting an exit interview where there is no hope of preventing the employee from leaving, as in this case, the longer the interview is delayed the more productive it is apt to be. This is because there is less employment time left for repercussions (as imagined by the employee) resulting from what might be revealed during the interview. The time of the interview was, therefore, set in the personnel officer's mind for Friday afternoon at 3:30—the employee's final employment hour on her last employment day. The interview was to be a surprise. This was to eliminate any buildup of apprehension which would only tend to reduce the effectiveness of the interview.

At three-thirty on Friday afternoon, Beverly was called to the personnel officer's office. When Beverly was seated, the officer sat back in his chair, looked Beverly straight in the eye and in a kindly voice asked, "Beverly, why are you really leaving the bank?" Beverly was a little startled. She regained her composure and began to relate how she had obtained another job offer by accident, and that it paid more money and appeared more challenging than her job at the bank. The officer then asked, "How did you get the job offer—by accident?" Beverly told a plausible story in reply. The officer then asked a question which did not logically follow from Beverly's previous remarks: "Had you been looking around a little for another job before this present offer?" Beverly answered, "Yes, a little." The officer again prodded in a searching voice, "Beverly, why are you really leaving the bank?" By this time, Beverly realized that the officer knew she had a story to tell and that he sincerely wanted to hear it. Beverly then blurted out, "I couldn't stand the pressure any more." Then she told her story. Her story was almost unbelievable, but it was supported with many examples of how poorly the manager treated her and the other employees. Her story took forty-five minutes to tell. It obviously had been bottled up inside her for several months. This interview released the pressure. Her thoughts literally cascaded from her mind. Partway through the interview the officer asked if it would be all right to take a few notes. When there was a natural pause in the conversation, the officer used his notes to clarify a point or to ask a sincere question to show his interest. This always encouraged Beverly to continue.

The interview ended somewhat sadly. Beverly admitted that she liked the bank very much, but she was leaving to get away from her manager. She even felt that if she had asked for and received a transfer to another department, her manager's influence with higher management would always adversely affect her career with the bank.

The comments made and the examples given by Beverly in her story were later checked by the officer and found to be true. Later, steps were taken to eliminate the problem.

This story illustrates the importance of learning the art of listening. If the officer had not been able to get Beverly to talk, he might never have learned of the seriousness of the problems in her department. Many more employees might have left the bank in the future because of mistreatment by this manager.

To learn is to learn to listen.

Summarizing and Following Through

Important oral communications require summarizing at the end of the communication and following through after the communication. The summary constitutes a verbal recap of the important points and the decisions made by both parties. The manager should make notes particularly on any decisions made. These notes will remind the manager of those items which need further action. They will also help in writing any permanent records that are required. When decisions are finalized in a communication, it is always important to follow through on the plan(s) of action decided upon. If, for example, it was decided to grant a certain day off to the employee a month from now, then a record of the date must be kept. Most decisions made, particularly many managerial decisions, are often in the form of promises. Promises are made to be kept, not forgotten. Employees will always remember unkept promises and will tend to be proportionately loyal to the manager in return.

Follow through may also require that the manager obtain additional facts about some important points mentioned in the communication before a decision is made. These facts have to be obtained and the decision then made and put into action.

Guidelines for Creative Group Meetings

In contrast to the usual type of employee meeting where the supervisor gives information to employees, the creative group meeting is designed to draw from the participants their ideas about a subject. Feedback, of course, is essential. Creative group meetings can be conducted successfully with employees, but only if the meeting is well organized. The following guidelines will be helpful in conducting a creative group employee meeting.

1. Limit the number of participants to five or six employees. A large number of employees often becomes too unwieldy for a supervisor to handle. The participants tend to form small groups and discuss topics among themselves instead of being a part of the whole group. A smaller number of employees (less than five) in the group could produce feedback problems. People tend to be inhibited if they are in a very small group.

2. Select employees for the meeting who are willing and able to speak and who have interest in and knowledge of the subject to be discussed.
3. Seat employees in a quiet environment—preferably at a round table to encourage a sense of equal status.
4. Confine each meeting to one topic of discussion so as not to fragment the discussion and dilute results. The topic, the reasons for discussing it, and its importance should be introduced at the beginning of the meeting.
5. Select relatively simple topics for discussion. Subjects such as solving temporary staffing problems, reducing expenses, increasing income, providing better customer service, and the developing of simpler job procedures are appropriate. Personnel-related departmental problems, such as those concerning tardiness, absenteeism, lack of cooperation, and the like, are best avoided because they often lead to the identification of specific employees who are causing the problems. Employees do not generally have enough experience to discuss these problems from a management point of view.
6. Permit participants to suggest ideas without criticism from either you or the other participants. Good ideas should be praised as such. This will encourage more ideas. Poor ideas or suggestions should be accepted gratefully but not commented upon negatively. Many apparently poor ideas have good parts to them which can be praised—for example, "I think we should have a suggestion box and award everyone making a suggestion five dollars," or "What we need is more space. We should build a new building," or "In order to provide better customer service, we should have guards or hostesses on duty each day to greet and direct customers." The supervisor could respond to these ideas with "Many corporations have had very good success with suggestion boxes. Perhaps we could offer a greater reward, but only for those suggestions accepted." "The lack of adequate space in our department has become acute recently. We should investigate acquiring space-saving filing equipment."

"Very good idea. Maybe we should start by having a hostess on duty at our busiest time—Saturday morning."

7. Do not dominate the discussion but rather lead the participants into discussion. After the subject of the discussion is introduced to the participants, the supervisor could advance two or three alternate ideas of his own and invite comments about these ideas. After a participant comments, ask questions about his ideas. This will generate more comments. Invite comments from all the other participants—"What do you think about that, Marion?"

8. At the end of the meeting, summarize important points made and courses of action decided upon. After the meeting, follow through with action on decisions made. If you do not follow through, the employees will think that the meeting was useless and will not be motivated to participate in future meetings.

Interviewing Job Applicants

Some banks require department supervisors to interview applicants for job openings that occur in their departments. These applicants usually have been screened by the personnel department and judged suitable for the openings. The theory behind this procedure is that the department manager, knowing exactly what the job requires and the personality mix of employees now working in the department, can better judge whether a specific applicant will fit into both the position and the department. Banks using this procedure generally give the manager the right to refuse any applicant he judges to be unacceptable. Allied to this procedure is the policy that requires managers to interview applicants for their job openings who are now working in other departments in the bank. These employees may be seeking a transfer or may have been approached by management to consider a transfer.

Even though banks may have different procedures for interviewing job applicants, department managers at least occasionally are required to interview prospective employees.

Therefore, they should know how to conduct meaningful interviews.

What to Look For

The whole purpose of job interviewing is to determine if the person applying for the job is suitable for the job. There are three criteria for determining the suitability of any applicant for any job opening—personality, proficiency and permanence.

Personality. The personal characteristics of the applicant must be matched with the job that is open and the employees who would be working closely with this person. Certain jobs require specific personal characteristics. Jobs involving a considerable amount of customer contact such as those in the tellers, new accounts, and customer service departments of a bank, for example, will require an applicant with a pleasant, outgoing, and mature personality. This will insure that the customer will always be treated courteously and that employees working in customer contact departments will not react adversely to the occasional irate or demanding customer. The shy, timid, and less mature applicant is more suitable for back office, non-customer contact positions such as those in the proof, bookkeeping, checkfile, stenographic, lock-box, mail, Brink's, record retention, and purchasing areas of the bank.

Matching an applicant's personal characteristics with those employees now working in the department is not as difficult as it may appear. People with differing or even opposite personal characteristics can and do work well together. There are some situations, however, that generally should be avoided—for example, placing a very youthful applicant with a number of older employees or vice versa, or placing a male applicant with a number of females or vice versa. These situations will not negatively affect the present employees in the department, but rather will in time affect the applicant. The applicant will have difficulty relating to the other employees because of differences in maturity and interests. The result of this mismatching is that the applicant will soon either request a transfer or just quit the job. Applicants with strong negative characteristics such as those who are highly irritable, emotionally unstable, or who have a constantly complaining nature should not be considered for employment in order to protect present employees from negative influences and to avoid supervisory problems for the manager.

Proficiency. The qualifications of the applicant must be matched with the duties of the job. These qualifications can be divided into three parts—education, work experience, and aptitude. Education and work experience are generally simple for the first-level manager to match with the duties of the job because most of the openings are beginning clerical jobs. These jobs usually require only a high-school level or equivalent education, and little or no work experience is often acceptable. Aptitude is the applicant's mental and physical ability to do a specific job, combined with interest in doing the job. Determining an applicant's abilities for and interest in a particular job can be difficult. In today's society, most mental ability and interest tests are considered inconclusive if not illegal. The only physical tests available that are reasonably conclusive for banking jobs are those used for measuring typing and shorthand skills. The manager, consequently, has to rely almost solely on the interview to determine the overall aptitude of an applicant.

Permanence. The applicant's potential longevity on the job and with the bank should be determined. Since the managers are interested in obtaining employees who will be permanent, they should identify those applicants who are looking for temporary or seasonal work or who may move out of the area in the near future. Caution: When determining in an interview the permanence of an applicant, remember that Equal Employment Opportunity laws prohibit employers from asking questions that would tend to discriminate. Accordingly, regardless of what is intended, questions concerning an applicant's transportation arrangements to or from work, babysitting plans, intentions to have children, or even whether a woman is pregnant or not are illegal. Also, the Age Discrimination in Employment Act prohibits discrimination because of age for those people who are between the ages of forty and seventy. If, for example your bank has a mandatory retirement age and you suspect that the applicant is close to this age, it would be illegal not to hire this person because of age. Questions concerning this applicant's age for any other reason would also be illegal.

The Interview

Through the interview the manager must determine, in what is usually a short period of time, the personality, proficiency, and permanence of the applicant. Once these characteristics are identified, then and only then can a definite decision be made about the applicant. To prepare and conduct a job interview, the manager should have in his possession an employment application or resume of the applicant's background. To attempt to interview without this written information is extremely difficult unless one is highly experienced in interviewing. Applications or resumes will give the manager a preview of the applicant's personal data (name, address, previous address, outside interests, and the like), work experience, and education. Applications or resumes should be reviewed by the manager before the interview to permit an adequate identification of those parts of the applicant's background that need further explanation.

The interview itself consists of four parts: the introduction, a discussion of the applicant's background, an explanation of the job opening, and the conclusion.

The introduction. This consists of the exchanging of names and general comments, or questions designed to relax the applicant. Statements like "It seems to be the coldest day of the year out there. Did you have trouble starting your car this morning?" or, "I see you live near me. Have you lived there for a long time?" are typical. The initial conversation with the applicant should establish a friendly unstrained rapport. It is important during this time not to allow first impressions to color one's judgments about the applicant. Keep an open mind until near the end of the interview. Some outstanding people give poor first impressions. Conversely, some people are skilled in giving good first impressions, but this veneer wears off as the interview progresses and the true personality emerges. Be careful not to judge a person by physical appearance. There is no correlation between a person's size, weight, hair, or skin coloring and his or her personality and aptitude. Each applicant is himself and unlike all others, and should be judged accordingly. A manager should, therefore, consider each interview a unique experience.

The discussion of the applicant's background. This is the heart of the interview and the opportunity for the manager to learn almost all that will be learned about the applicant's personality, proficiency, and permanence. If for some reason the application or resume could not be reviewed before, it is important that the manager take the time to read it before the discussion of the applicant's background begins. Merely explain to the applicant that you would like to take a few minutes to review the application. Then read the whole thing through before asking questions. A discussion of the applicant's background can be divided into three parts—personal data, education, and work experience. With regard to an applicant's personal data, regardless of what might appear on the application, avoid all questions and comments about an applicant's age, sex, marital status, dependents, race, national origin, and religious beliefs and affiliations. As was mentioned before, this includes questions or comments about transportation to work, babysitting arrangements, and the applicant's plans for having children. Questions about a person's current and previous address, and questions about an applicant's hobbies and sport interests are acceptable. Short conversations about a person's outside interests will tend to relax the applicant and encourage him to talk. The more he talks the more his personality will be revealed.

Most of the discussion about an applicant's background will center around the person's education and work background. The first thing for a manager to establish in his mind is a history of the applicant's activity from the time he left high school until the present time. Any lapses in school or work time, even for two or three months, should be identified and understood. Applicants who jump from school to school, job to job, place to place, or who go on frequent vacation trips of one month or longer are not apt to be permanent employees. Determining a recent high school graduate's permanence, for example, is difficult. Questions like "Do you plan to continue your education in some way?" and "Do you plan to move out of the area in the near future?" will help. If the young applicant has been living in the area for several years, he is more apt to stay in the area. If the young applicant has just moved into the area from a distant place that was his home, then the reason for the move should be investigated thoroughly. Any reasons for moving into a new area should be investigated.

The following sample questions about the applicant's education and work experience (including work interests and aptitudes) will be helpful in determining his personality, proficiency, and permanence—all of which then can easily be related to the job opening. These questions should be asked after the manager has determined the history of the applicant's activity since high school.

About education:

1. What were your grades in high school?
2. Have you had any education beyond high school?
3. What were your grades in college?
4. What courses did you like best? Why? What were your grades in those courses?
5. What courses did you like least? Why?
6. Do you remember your rank in high school? In college?
7. Did you receive any special honors? What were they?
8. In what extra-curricular activities did you participate in high school? In college?
9. What was your major course of study in college? Why did you choose it?
10. Have you had any college business courses?
11. Did you receive a college degree? If not, why did you leave school before receiving your degree?
12. Do you plan to further your education?

About work experience and work interests:

1. What type of work did you do in your last job?
2. Why are you thinking about leaving, or why did you leave? If appropriate, ask the applicant why he left all previous jobs.
3. What did you like best about your previous job? Why?
4. What did you like least in your previous job? Why?
5. Were you promoted or transferred in any of the companies where you worked?
6. What was your starting salary in your last job? What is your present salary?
7. What kind of reference do you think your previous boss will give you?
8. What attracts you to banking?
9. What type of work would you really like to do if you had your choice of working in any profession or in any job in the country?
10. Do you like working with numbers? Would you estimate that you have below average, average, or above average figure ability?
11. Do you like working with people?
12. Can you operate any business machines?
13. Have you had any experience with the public? In person? On the telephone?
14. Do you like people?
15. Do you like to work by yourself in a semi-isolated environment?
16. What specific things are you looking for in your next job?
17. What are your short and long range job goals?

These sample questions are presented as tools to help the manager engage in an information-gathering conversation. They should not be asked one after another as if they were rehearsed and are being presented by a machine. Even though some of the answers to these questions may appear on the application, a manager can and often should ask the applicant again for a verbal response. The verbal response will encourage conversation and may provide the manager with more exact information. Some managers may be reticent to ask some of these questions because it would be obvious to the applicant why the question is being asked. They think the answers might be more in accordance with what the manager wants to hear rather than the actual truth. The vast majority of applicants will not lie in response to these questions but rather will at most only shade the truth or avoid a direct answer. Managers will have to *listen* carefully to the answers. Listening to the choice of words, for hesitations in the applicant's voice, and to the content of the answer is important in determining if the answer has been either shaded to favor the applicant's background or answered in complete honesty. Surprisingly, many applicants are hesitant to talk about their accomplishments because of humility or for fear of being labeled by the interviewer as a braggart. If the manager suspects either overstatements or understatements of abilities, he should probe deeper to determine the truth.

Since direct aptitude tests for most bank jobs are either not available or illegal to administer, the direct questioning technique is valuable and should be used. General questions concerning a person's finger dexterity, figure ability, business machine orientation, and ability to do routine filing, sorting, or counting work will be answered truthfully by the applicant to the best of his ability. No one, unless he is absolutely desperate for a job, will want a job that he knows he is not capable of doing because, once he is on the job, the manager is going to find out about his lack of aptitude anyway.

When matching the educational and work background of an applicant to a job opening, it is just as important to be concerned about the overqualified applicant as it is to be about the obvious problem presented in the underqualified applicant. Hiring an overqualified person can cause a permanency problem after a few months of employment. A sharp young college graduate being considered for a teller job or a bright twenty-year-old applicant with three years of proof machine experience applying for a proof operator's job are, for example, potential permanency problems. These applicants may be interested in obtaining a job to get immediate income. After a few months, however, they may become bored and start looking for advancement or a transfer to a different job. If a change in assignment does not come, they will often become dejected and disappointed with what they view as a lack of job growth. This in turn could lead to their eventual termination from their jobs.

Managers must also be careful of the applicant who has been used to earning a salary much higher than the salary level of the job opening. There are exceptions, but most people, after they are on the job for awhile, become dissatisfied with their salary level, and discouraged when they compare their present salary to their previous high salary. And so the manager must determine most accurately, through questioning, the motives of overqualified people who apply for a job.

Explanation of the job opening. This can be a short or long explanation depending on the manager's interest in hiring the applicant. An up-to-date written job description is very helpful in explaining the duties of the job. This explanation, however, should include the working hours, the number of days in the work week, the starting salary and the salary review schedule. A tour of the department pointing out the location of the job that is open and a brief demonstration of any banking machines used in the job are very informative for the applicant. Finally, particularly for someone new to banking, a short talk about the universality of the banking profession, the growth and position of the bank in the community, and the educational and promotional opportunities available is appropriate. When describing the duties of the job and all the other related subjects, it is important to be accurate. The applicant should be correctly informed about the job and all its aspects. The facts should neither be overstated nor understated; nor should any important facts be omitted. If the manager is interested in the applicant, a complete explanation of the job will give the applicant sufficient knowledge to make an intelligent decision. The possibility of an applicant accepting a position that would not be suited for him is therefore greatly reduced.

The conclusion. At the end of the interview, the manager will have arrived at a judgment about the applicant. Either he is interested in hiring the applicant, not interested, or not sure. If the manager is not sure about an applicant for good, definable reasons, or even for strong, undefinable feelings, the applicant should be put into the not-interested catagory. The manager should never hire anybody when there are serious doubts. Also, he should never lower his normal standards out of desperation for help. The person hired out of desperation generally will cause longer-lived desperation in the days and months to come.

If there is a high degree of interest in hiring the applicant, it should be mentioned to the applicant before the interview is over. The manager should ask the applicant if he is interested in the job. The job offer, in most instances, should not be made at the interview. Sufficient time should be allowed (but usually not more than twenty-four hours for clerical employees) for both the manager and the applicant to solidify their mutual interest. This will also allow sufficient time to check the necessary references before a final job offer is made. The applicant should be told that he will be contacted within twenty-four hours. Delaying a job offer to an applicant for whom there is a high degree of interest for longer than twenty-four hours will sharply increase the possibility that the applicant will be offered another job. Good applicants are in demand and, if not hired soon after the interview by your bank, will certainly be hired by another company.

To conclude an interview with an applicant in whom there is doubtful interest or no interest at all, the manager can inform the applicant that there have been others who have applied for the job who will be also considered, or that other applicants have been scheduled to be interviewed for the opening and they will be interviewed before a final decision is made. The applicant should also be told that, if he has not been contacted by the bank within three or four days, he should conclude that no job offer will be made at this time. In some instances an applicant should be told during the interview that a job offer will not be made. Typical of these situations is when an applicant is underqualified, has too high a salary requirement, or is not able to work during the hours required.

The length of the interview is determined by the interest level the manager has for the applicant. The whole interviewing process can be shortened considerably if the interest level is low. Fewer questions are asked about the applicant's background, and shorter explanations are given about the job duties.

Regardless of the interest level the manager has for the applicant, the applicant should always be treated in a friendly and courteous manner—as if he or she were a customer of the bank. Applicants will relate to their friends and relatives the favorable and the unfavorable interviews that they have experienced, and the bank's reputation will be enhanced or diminished accordingly.

III

Organizing, Planning, Delegating

To organize is to put in order. The world we live in is a study in order. The stars and planets move through the universe in precise, predictable order. The earth rotates and moves around the sun to create our days and nights and seasons of the year —all in perfect order. The balance of nature in the numbers and kinds of plants and animals on the earth suggests order. People, therefore, who live in a natural world of order, desire to direct their daily efforts according to an orderly plan. And only through order are things accomplished. History records countless seemingly impossible tasks that could only have come about because people have the ability to organize their efforts toward accomplishing a goal.

The great Egyptian pyramid of Giza which covers thirteen acres was constructed by an army of workers who quarried, transported and put into place the astonishing total of 2,300,000 huge blocks of granite and limestone. In late October in the year 218 B.C., Hannibal, the great Carthaginian general, began the incredible task of moving an army of about 38,000 men, 9,000 horses, and 38 elephants across the Alps. Fifteen days later, after fighting snow, ice, cold, hunger, and bands of hostile tribesmen, Hannibal and his army descended into Italy to win several major battles against the Romans. Today, by coordinating the resources and technology of many industries, we send both people and machines out into space to explore our solar system.

These accomplishments required the coordination of the talents and efforts of many people. And coordinating the work efforts of people requires organization—planning, staffing, scheduling, and delegating.

Organizational Structure

All organizations are composed of units of employees arranged according to work functions. In banks these units are basically divided into three types—sections, departments, and divisions. Sections are the parts of a department. Departments are the parts of a division. Divisions are the main parts of a bank. An organizational chart can be drawn to show this structure. The chart shows how the various sections, departments, and divisions of a bank are arranged according to functions. Organizational charts often show the names and titles of those persons in charge of each function. By viewing the chart, it is simple to determine the functions for which each manager is responsible and to identify the individual to whom each manager reports.

Figure 2 shows a simplified organizational chart for a medium-size bank. The chart shows that the bank is organized into five divisions—operations, control, loans, trust, and branch administration. Each division officer reports to the president. Each department supervisor reports to his respective division manager. All persons shown on the chart regardless of their title are managers. The division managers have more responsibility than the department managers. The division managers, therefore, along with the chairman of the board and the president, constitute the senior management of the bank. In this bank there is a definite chain of command. Each manager knows who his boss is and the functions for which he or she is responsible. Roy Davis, manager of the note department, for example, reports to Joseph Raden who reports to Herbert Steele who reports to the president, Mr. Jones. Each manager manages his own department or division and has no authority over any other department or division.

Figure 2
Bank Organization Chart

```
┌──────────────┐
│ Stockholders │
└──────┬───────┘
       │
┌──────┴───────┐
│Board of      │
│Directors     │
└──────┬───────┘
       │
┌──────┴────────────┐
│Chairman of the    │
│Board              │
│Joseph A. Stone    │
└──────┬────────────┘
       │
┌──────┴────────────┐
│President          │
│H. James Jones     │
└──────┬────────────┘
```

Operations Division — Mary S. Watson — Vice-President and Cashier
- Teller Dept. — Sonja L. Swanson — Ass't Cashier
- Customer Serv. Dept. — Dennis Calhoun — Ass't Vice-President
- Proof/Bookkeeping Dept. — Ronald Tate — Ass't Cashier

Control Divison — Georgia Stone — Vice-President and Controller

Loan Division — Herbert L. Steele — Senior Vice-President
- Installment Loan Dept. — Alice R. Howard — Ass't Vice-President
- Commercial Loan Dept. — Joseph Raden — Vice-President
- Mortgage Loan Dept. — Glenn O'Malley — Manager
- Note Dept. — Roy D. Davis — Manager

Trust Division — William D. Conrad — Vice-President and Trust Officer

Branch Administration Division — Donald F. Schwartz — Vice-President
- West Branch — Ann T. Jansen — Manager
- South Branch — Robert Mott — Manager
- North Branch — Terry O'Toole — Ass't Vice-President

It is important that managers, regardless of their positions, follow the chain of command when directing the daily activities of the bank. If, for example, Georgia Stone, vice president and controller, happens to be walking through the bank lobby one day and she notices that a customer was not properly serviced by a teller, she should not take it upon herself to instruct or criticize the teller. Rather, she should mention the incident to Mary Watson, vice president in charge of the operations division. In Mary Watson's absence she should speak to Sonja Swanson, who manages the teller department and who in turn will contact the teller. Following the chain of command in all management situations has two main advantages. It keeps the division and departmental managers informed about what is going on in their areas of responsibility, and it protects the organizational structure from disintegrating into a chaotic managerial environment in which employees are not sure to whom they are responsible. When employees feel they have too many bosses, they often respond in a disinterested, confused, and uncooperative manner. *One boss is enough for any employee.*

Organizational structure should exist also at the departmental level. Jobs within a department that directly relate to one another should be organized into sections. Figure 3 shows an organizational chart for the teller department of our typical, medium-size bank. This department is organized into six sections. Sonja Swanson is the manager of the department and Rachel Gordon is her assistant. The various supervisors and senior tellers, in addition to substituting as tellers when needed, help Sonja and Rachel in the day-to-day activities of their respective sections. They approve checks, schedule tellers, investigate discrepancies, balance tellers, order cash, train new tellers, etc.

In a growing department where the number of employees is continually becoming larger, a manager must be aware of the number of employees reporting directly to him. In busy bank operating departments, particularly if the manager must also on occasion service customers, the ideal number of employees who should be reporting to one person is ten. Ten to twelve

Figure 3
Department Organization Chart

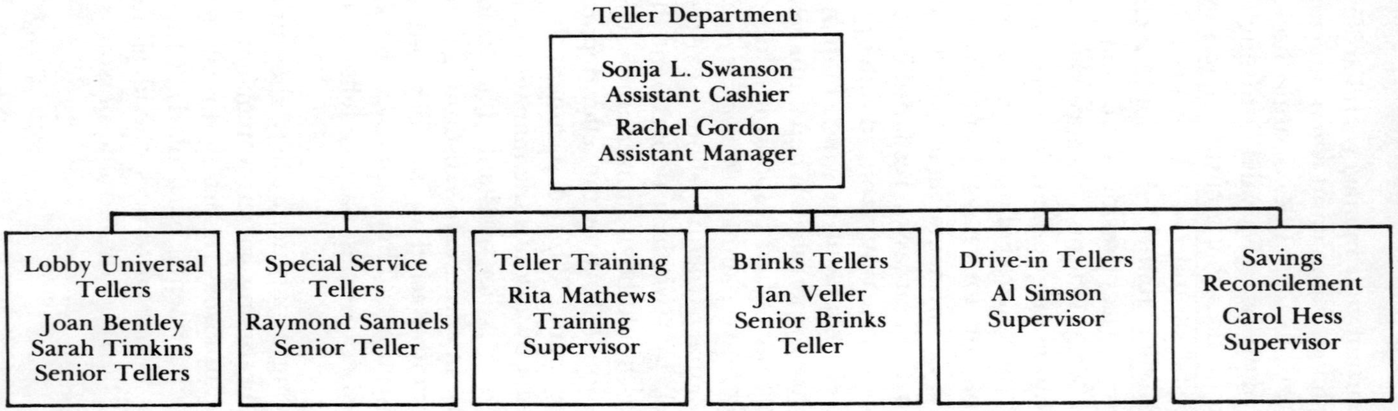

Teller Department

Sonja L. Swanson
Assistant Cashier
Rachel Gordon
Assistant Manager

Lobby Universal
Tellers
Joan Bentley
Sarah Timkins
Senior Tellers

Special Service
Tellers
Raymond Samuels
Senior Teller

Teller Training
Rita Mathews
Training
Supervisor

Brinks Tellers
Jan Veller
Senior Brinks
Teller

Drive-in Tellers
Al Simson
Supervisor

Savings
Reconcilement
Carol Hess
Supervisor

employees per manager is what is called the optimum span of control. If a manager is required to manage directly the activities of more than this number of employees, then the span of control is too large for one manager to handle on a day to-day basis. Effectiveness in the management of each employee will be reduced in direct relation to the increase in the number of employees to be managed. Without managerial help of some kind (an assistant manager, section supervisors, etc.) the manager will soon begin to see erosion in the efficiency with which the department operates. Employees will be less adequately trained in their jobs, they will perform their duties less accurately, and they will waste more time on the job. The manager will spend more and more of his time on minor managerial tasks such as organizing daily schedules, solving small customer and employee complaints, performing clerical functions, etc. Less and less time will be spent by the manager on the more important managerial functions of organizing, communicating, training, and motivating.

Planning

To plan is to have the ability to anticipate the future. All plans are made for future courses of action. Banks, like all businesses, operate in a changing environment. New bank services are added each year. Equipment becomes obsolete or worn out. New departments or sections are created. Existing departments grow in size. The functions of departments become more complex. Better bank operating procedures are developed each year. Because of natural turnover, transfers and promotions, the nature of the employees working in a department or section often changes. All of this, in addition to the day-to-day activities of staffing and scheduling, requires planning. Planning is the use of imagination to anticipate future needs in relation to the present environment and then to plot a course of action to meet those needs.

A supervisor cannot afford to wait for the future to arrive without planning for it. The result of lack of planning is chaos.

If, for example, the supervisor of a teller department does not anticipate the Monday volume after a three-day holiday weekend and schedule enough tellers to be on duty, Monday will arrive and customers will be "lined out to the streets." The drive-in teller lanes will be jammed with cars. Customers will be complaining. Senior management will be complaining. Overworked tellers will be complaining. The result—chaos!

Managers must plan for equipment needs, departmental growth, staff changes, new services, volume variances, space requirements, changes in operating procedures, and new banking trends. It is never too soon to plan for the future in banking.

How to Plan

After knowing what has to be planned, the second phase of planning is to know how to plan. Two important tools used by the planner are pencil and paper! There is magic in the process of expressing one's thoughts on paper. Writing forces the mind to think, to organize, to put the abstract into the concrete. It records thoughts that may be forgotten. It generates more thought which in turn leads to the development of more choices, more solutions, and the awareness of important, but often overlooked, parts of the project.

Also important in knowing how to plan is knowing what questions to ask. There are three quesitons which a manager has to ask with regard to planning: What are the parts of the project? When do they have to be done? Who is going to do them?

In order to illustrate the process of planning, let us assume that the vice president in charge of operations has just given the manager of the teller department the assignment of converting the bank's 10,000 checking-account signature cards, and 10,000 savings-account signature cards, and all future new-account signature cards to microfiche. It is assumed that the vice president knows the approximate costs involved and has approved this expenditure. It is assumed also that the vice president has already determined the time and space-saving advantages of reducing the 20,000 signature cards to a file containing only thirty three-by-five-inch microfiche records. The manager has been directed to complete this project as soon as possible. Three steps are involved.

1. Write down the parts of the project.
2. Write down when they have to be done.
3. Write down who is going to do them.

Write down the parts of the project. At this point the manager may be saying to himself, "I've never even seen a signature card on microfiche let alone know how to convert 20,000 cards to this system!" The first part of the project, therefore, is to visit a bank that has its signature cards on microfiche. After visiting that bank, the other major parts of the project will become apparent and so, for the time being, they can be listed at random as they are determined. Shown below is a sample listing of the major parts of this project.

1. Visit banks.
2. Research companies that will convert present signature cards to microfiche and that will put future new account cards on the system after present file is converted.
3. Research companies that sell microfiche viewers. Determine the number of viewers needed.
4. Sign contract for converting cards. Determine conversion date.
5. Order viewers. Determine delivery date.
6. Develop plans in preparation for conversion by determining answers to the following questions.
    a. How will locator numbers be assigned?
    b. Will both sides of cards be put on the microfiche?
    c. Where will cards be converted? How long will it take? How will tellers operate while cards are being filmed?
    d. If an account has more than one card, will all cards be filmed?
    e. Will checking and savings cards be intermingled on microfiche?

     f. How many sets of microfiche will be required? Should they be color coded to distinguish them from other records already on microfiche?

7. Develop operating plan to put subsequent new-account signature cards on microfiche after present cards are converted by answering the following questions.
    a. How often will file be updated? How long will it take?
    b. If cards will be filmed off the premises, how will tellers look up the signatures of new-account customers?
    c. Who will be assigned the job of updating these new account cards? How will this employee be trained?
8. Convert cards and start updating system.
9. Train tellers to use this new system.

Write down when the parts of the project will be completed and who is going to do them. In the early twentieth century, Henry L. Gantt developed a simple time chart that helps managers document the parts of a project. By completing this chart a manager can determine more easily when each part of the project should start, how long it will take to complete it, when it will be completed, and how it relates in time to the other parts. Figure 4 shows a Gantt Chart for the nine major parts of the microfiche signature-card project. A "who" column was added to this chart in order to list conveniently the names of those responsible for completing each part of the project. The chart can be set up near the beginning of the project and adjusted as required when all the facts have been determined. The chart can also be used as a schedule from which the manager can easily determine whether each part of the project is being completed on time as planned.

Time Planning for Managers

A common complaint voiced by many first-level bank managers is that they do not have enough time to accomplish such important parts of the managerial job as training, communicat-

Figure 4
Gantt Chart—Conversion of Checking and Saving Account Signature Cards to Microfiche

Parts of the Project	First Week	Second Week	Third Week	Fourth Week	Fifth Week	Sixth Week	Seventh Week	Eighth Week	Ninth Week	Who
1. Visit banks	■	■								Manager
2. Research companies for conversion		■	■	■						Manager
3. Research companies for viewers		■	■	■						Manager and Assistant Manager
4. Sign contracts-conversion date				■				■		Manager
5. Order viewers-delivery date				■			■			Manager
6. Develop plans for conversion					■	■	■			Manager and Assistant Manager
7. Develop plan for updating file					■	■	■			Assistant Manager
8. Convert files and start updating								■	■	Manager and Assistant Manager
9. Train Tellers								■	■	Training Supervisor

ing with, and motivating their employees. Assuming that a manager is sincere about performing these managerial functions, the problem of "not enough time" usually comes down to the manager's inability to plan his time. There always must be enough time for the important managerial duties. Time planning can be considered from two aspects—conserving time, and making the best use of the time available. In order to conserve time, "time wasters" have to be identified and eliminated from the manager's workday. The following major "time wasters" are common to the bank manager.

The tendency towards trivia. A manager is often tempted to involve himself in the routine detail work; perhaps this is a vestige of his earlier, non-managerial jobs. The theory "I'll do it myself rather than show someone else how to do it—it's faster" is a false supposition. Routine filing, report preparation, investigating, counting, sorting, and recording are jobs that occur every day. Once they are taught to others, these daily time-consuming jobs are eliminated forever from the manager's work day. Managers often bury themselves in this type of work because they feel that they must be busy all the time to make a good impression on their employees or higher management. Clerical work is seen as an easy way to keep busy. But it is much more profitable to be busy devising a better system to train employees or to motivate them toward being more productive in their jobs. The manager is not obligated to impress employees with the quantity of routine work that can be performed, but rather to impress higher management with what major accomplishments the department has produced in a given period of time. The inability to delegate non-management functions to others is another reason for the tendency towards trivia. The subject of delegation is discussed later in this chapter.

Interruptions. Phone calls, questions, approvals, customer inquiries, visitors, and socializing are often unnecessary sources of interruptions. Analyze the phone calls. Are many of them misdirected? If so, inform the person who is misdirecting them. Can someone answer your phone when you are busy? Assign someone to take messages or ask if they can help. Do the employees ask too many oversimplified questions? Train them to answer their own questions. Do employees bring too many items to you for approval? Examine your approval limits. Are you located physically too near the customers in the lobby where you are constantly interrupted by routine questions? Are you located in a central area where employees from other departments can easily stop by on their way for a visit? Move to a more isolated location. Are you besieged with unwanted salesmen? Say no before they come to your desk.

Fire fighting. Some managers operate by solving one crisis after another. They are constantly running around the department solving employee problems, placating customers, hurriedly completing overdue reports, or switching employees around at the last minute to solve a temporary staffing problem. This type of management—called fire-fighting management or crisis management—is often rooted in the manager's inability to anticipate the future and thus plan courses of action which reduce the possibility of constant crises. Fire-fighting management is extremely time consuming. It is much easier to prevent a fire through proper planning than to fight a fire.

Procrastination. There are some unpleasant but necessary jobs involving people which managers have to do. Procrastinating about calling back an irate customer, refusing an employee a salary raise, or talking to the boss about a serious loss that occurred is a time waster because it preys upon the manager's mind—often to the exclusion of other duties. The best way to handle these situations is to take care of them quickly. Get them over with and thereby free the mind for other things.

Once the time wasters have been eliminated, the time made available has to be planned in order to accomplish objectives. As mentioned before, the tools of a planner are pencil and paper. The major objectives for each day should be noted in order of importance before each day begins. The most important objectives are to be accomplished first, even if the other, less important items remain untouched. Only through an orderly approach to time planning will objectives be accomplished. By writing down objectives, the mind is forced to organize and plan each day's activities. The written list also serves as a constant reminder of what has to be done. The following points will be helpful in accomplishing daily objectives.

1. Remember that only results count. Activity is only a means to accomplish an end. The project should be finished. Finished projects build confidence.
2. All large projects are made up of small parts. Divide the project into workable parts and then consider each part as a daily objective. Thinking about doing the project in its totality can be discouraging.
3. Beware of the trap of finishing less important projects so that you will have time to start on the important one. Do the important one first. Do the unimportant ones some other time. Follow priorities.
4. Be careful of perfectionism. Working on a project until it is absolutely perfect is a luxury that few can afford. The absolute perfectionist accomplishes only a few things when he may have many things to do.
5. Set deadlines for projects and write them down. If the projects are large, announce your deadlines to others such as your boss or peer managers. These actions are commitments. Written and announced commitments are hard to break.
6. Identify those blocks of time during the day that for you are relatively free from interruptions. Plan to do your important projects during those times.
7. Fire up your interest in a project by doing the required research. This investigative process will excite your curiosity and build up your ambition for starting the job.

Planning Employees' Time

Employees are not usually expected to be planners of their time. Managers, therefore, must not only plan their own time but also their employees' time. The three major wasters of employees' time are lack of organization in job duties, poor employee training, and interruptions.

Managers must know well the duties of each departmental job and how long it normally should take to perform these duties. Written job descriptions define job duties in an organized manner; they are very helpful in pinpointing the exact duties of each job. The continual updating of existing job descriptions will insure against the possibility of employees performing duties which are no longer required. Typical of this in banks is the preparation of reports which, although important when first instituted, often have no current value to anyone. Determining the time required to perform the duties of each job requires that a manager compare, through experience, the performance of others who have done the same duties in the past with those who presently perform these functions. Accumulating statistical records with regard to volume of items processed, number of customers serviced, and the number of customer accounts is of paramount importance. These statistics will provide the manager with an ongoing report of the volume processed by employees, and also a basis on which to compare the time required to process work with other banks in the area. The value of accumulating and interpreting pertinent statistical information cannot be overemphasized as it relates to planning employees' time. A more detailed explanation regarding the proper method of accumulating and interpreting departmental statistical information is presented in chapter 7 of this book.

Armed with job descriptions and statistics on the time required to perform these duties, the supervisor will be in a position to plan employees' time and eliminate wasted time. If left to their own devices, some employees will fill an eight-hour day with six hours of work, while others might attempt to compress ten hours of work into an eight-hour day. The time wasted in the former and the frustrations generated by the latter are apparent.

Poor employee training is another employee time-waster. Consider all those clerical jobs of adding, counting, sorting, and filing that employees do hour after hour. There is a correct, time-efficient way to perform each of these jobs. Employees should be trained properly from the beginning. Left on their own they will perform these jobs according to their own systems developed through trial and error. They will function without the benefit of knowing the most time-efficient way to perform these jobs as developed through the past experience of others. How much time is wasted, for example, by the poorly trained file clerk who files cards into an alphabetic file without first putting the cards to be filed in alphabetic order? How much time is wasted by the proof operator of a ten key machine who indexes amounts with one finger? How much time is wasted by the typist who uses two fingers on the typewriter?

Finally, interruptions are thieves of time. Personal telephone calls, socializing, equipment breakdowns, and unnecessary interruptions by the manager are typical. Allied to these are the extended lunch hour or coffee break and undefined daily starting or ending times. Socializing by two or more employees has a multiplying effect. Time is wasted by all employees involved in the conversation and even by those nearby who might be tempted to interrupt their work to listen to the conversation. Managers seldom think of themselves as possible interruptions in the daily duties of employees, but they should identify those communications that have to be made while the employee is working intently from those which can be deferred easily until a time when there is a natural break in the work. Necessary but emotionally disturbing conversations with employees about poor job performance, excessive absenteeism, salary raise denials, etc., should be deferred until the end of the work day. In more serious situations they should be put off until the end of the work week. This gives employees time to gain composure during non-working hours. It eliminates the possibility of their wasting time worrying or thinking about the unpleasant conversation when they should be concentrating on their work.

Staffing

A major planning function of the bank supervisor is the staffing of a department with the proper number of employees at all times. For a supervisor in a bank operating department, this can be complex. As in all planning activities, staffing requires anticipating future needs. In planning for temporary volume increases or staff shortages, the causes should be determined in advance and planned for accordingly. Temporary volume increases in a bank traditionally occur during the beginning and end of the week, the first and the fifteenth of the month, the days before and particularly after holidays, savings account interest-posting periods, social security payment days, and other large pay days.

General activity in a bank is slower during the winter months starting about the fifteenth of January, and remaining so until the end of March. From April first, activity will build to a peak in July, drop a little in August and will remain at a high level until the following January. Temporary staff shortages occur during times of excessive employee turnover, employee vacation periods, and abnormal employee absenteeism. Increases in the normal absenteeism rate usually occur during the spring and fall of the year when colds, flus and viral illnesses are more prevalent. Often, temporary volume increases and staff shortages occur at the same time. This causes even more acute staffing problems if not planned for well in advance.

Planning for temporary volume increases and staff shortages requires constant planning for the future. A vital tool for this type of planning is a calendar which shows all the days of the month on one sheet of paper with space under each day to write notes. All known potential problems together with possible solutions can be recorded on this calendar a month in advance. As the month progresses, new situations can be recorded too. This type of calendar gives the manager a snapshot view at any time of what will be happening and what plans have to be made.

The regular staff of a department can handle the volume fluctuations as they occur during the year provided that the supervisor has not aggravated the situation by granting too much time off for vacations or other special reasons during these periods. Occasionally the staffing problem will become acute because many things which are beyond the control of the supervisor happen at the same time. To solve these staffing problems, the following alternatives are available.

1. Ask regular full-time employees if they would be willing to work extra hours for additional pay. Most employees will cooperate if they are given three or four days notice,

if the number of extra hours is not excessive, and if the duration of the problem is not long (one to two days of extra hours). If the problem will exist for a week, for example, some employees could work extra hours on Monday and Wednesday and others on Tuesday and Thursday.

2. Ask those employees who are scheduled for vacation if they can defer it. The more notice given for this request, the better the chance the employee will be willing to cooperate—particularly if firm plans for leaving town have not been made.

3. Ask part-time employees if they could work extra days or parts of a day or extra hours depending on the situation. Often a temporary staffing problem which will short a small department one person for a day can be solved by obtaining help for part of a day (such as during lunch hour).

4. Ask for temporary help from another department. Employees who have worked in one department and have been permanently transferred to another department often find it enjoyable to help out in their old department for a day or two.

5. Ask shift employees who normally work one shift if they could work a few additional hours for pay on another shift.

The above alternatives are available only if a supervisor has planned well, knows in advance that the problem will exist, and provides for the solution in advance. A supervisor who does not plan well won't realize the problem until it is well upon him, and he will be forced to engage in crisis management much to the consternation of both himself and the employees.

Staffing for permanent shortages, such as those caused by increased volume, turnover, new services, and the like, can be done a variety of ways other than the obvious one of hiring additional full-time employees. Each time there is an apparent need for help in a department, even due to natural turnover, the work that is now being done by employees should be analyzed. Can present jobs now being done by several people be combined? Can some duties in certain jobs be eliminated? Should duties in several different jobs be rearranged and included in other jobs? Once these questions are answered and more help is still indicated, then the search for additional help can begin. The hiring of employees is normally a function of the personnel officer. The supervisor, however, can inquire about or recommend present part-time employees who may wish to work more hours on a permanent basis, or past part-time or full-time employees who left the bank for unavoidable reasons and may wish to return to work. If these alternatives prove fruitless, then new part-time or full-time employees have to be hired.

Managers always have to be alert against long-term understaffing or overstaffing. Understaffing a department for any length of time will result in employees working longer hours and that eventually leads to morale problems and increased turnover. Understaffing can be avoided by continually reviewing the effects which increased volume, the addition of services, increases in the number of holidays, vacations, sick leaves, and extension of banking hours have on the department. Overstaffing, in addition to the obvious costs involved, will slow down the pace of the employees to below standard. Once this pace has been reduced, it automatically becomes standard in the eyes of the employees, and future attempts by the manager to increase this pace will be difficult to effect. Overstaffing can be avoided by never adding to staff without a good reason that is based on facts and not feelings. Correctly planning employee time and reviewing statistical information regarding work volumes are excellent ways to maintain a correctly staffed department.

Delegating

Perhaps one of the most difficult things for managers to do is to delegate. Delegation is assigning to someone else nonmanagerial jobs that are now being done by the manager. The manager's job is to get things done through other people. To do this a manager must communicate well with employees, organize, train, and motivate them. To perform these functions well is a full-time job. Delegation is an organizational function of management that is fundamental because it is the only way to get things done through other people. The manager who does not delegate will never have enough time to do his own job. He will be too busy doing those jobs that should be done by others.

Reasons Why Managers Don't Delegate

Don't know how to delegate. Delegation is a function of management which can be learned. The subject of how to delegate is presented later in this chapter.

Fear of employees' reactions. There is often the fear that the employee will be thinking "Why doesn't the manager do it?" This is especially the fear of new managers. It is usually a product of manager's insecurity in his new role as one who gets things done through other people, and the employees' incorrect view that managers are super workers. Once employees become familiar with the correct function of management—the direction of the efforts of others as consistently practiced by the manager—their misunderstandings will disappear.

Fear of having too much time with nothing to do. This is a misconceived fear that derives either from the manager's unwillingness to perform as a manager or from his ignorance of the management function. Any manager who fully understands the principles of management and operates accordingly will never be idle.

Fear of the quality of work of the delegatee. This fear can work in two ways. If the person to whom the work is delegated does a good job, then the fear is that the worker will be better than the manager. If the delegatee does a poor job, then the fear is that this will reflect the manager's inability to get the work done properly. In the former instance, managers must realize that they have been placed in their jobs not because they are super check filers, super proof operators, super tellers, or super clerks, but rather because they showed talent for being super directors, super organizers, super trainers, super communicators, super motivators, etc. Accordingly, a good performance on the part of the delegatee will reflect on the manager's good judgement in selecting that delegatee for the job.

A manager who matches the work to be done with the abilities of the delegatee and who then watches the performance of the employee carefully during early stages of the job has little to fear. By watching the employee in the early stages after the work is delegated, a manager can always determine within a short period of time if the job was delegated to the wrong person. No delegation decision is irrevocable. The delegatee can be reassigned to different work before any disaster befalls the department. There is always some risk in any decision a manager may make. But by making decisions properly, the risks are always reduced to a minimum. (The subject of decision making is presented in the next chapter.)

Belief that there is no one to whom to delegate. If the manager is planning employee time and staffing the department in accordance with the principles of time planning and staffing presented earlier in this chapter, then there is *always* someone to whom to delegate the work.

Belief that it is easier to do the work than to take the time to train someone else. This is a false assumption that is based on expediency. Expediency dictates that one take advantage of the opportunity to do the job to get it done rather than take considerably more time to train someone else to do it. But work that usually is delegated is repetitive in nature. Accordingly, the work has to be done again and again, perhaps twenty times a day or twenty times a week. Regardless of how often it has to be done, once it is learned by another it never has to be done again by the manager.

Desire to do the work. A manager often has the desire to do a particular job even though the work could and should be delegated to someone else. This desire comes perhaps from the manager's enjoyment of and satisfaction in doing the work, or from the erroneous belief that no one can really do it as well or as efficiently as he can. Regardless of the reason, a manager has to realize that he cannot afford the luxury (in terms of time) of doing things that should be delegated. New interests and satisfactions await the manager in performing management functions. And there is always someone else who is capable of doing the job well.

How to Delegate

To delegate effectively, the knowledge of only two principles is required—what to delegate and to whom to delegate. In identifying what to delegate, the supervisor should have as his goal the delegation to others of all those duties which are not directly related to management. Routine or even sporadic clerical duties, therefore, such as filing, counting, sorting, recording, completing forms, operating business machines, preparing routine reports, and searching through records should be delegated. Making minor decisions and answering routine questions should be included in the list of things to be delegated. Bank managers are besieged each day with a variety of matters requiring minor decisions. Typical of these situations are those regarding check approvals, service charge rebates, waiving bank charges, and solving minor staffing problems. The majority of routine questions asked of a bank manager by employees are either questions asked through the employee by a customer or procedural questions. Customers either on the telephone or in person ask employees questions about their accounts or other bank services. The employees often rely too heavily on the supervisor to answer these questions. Employees also ask procedural questions about their daily work often to a point of using the manager as a crutch.

After the jobs that should be delegated have been identified—namely clerical work, making minor decisions, and answering routine questions—the next step is to determine to whom to delegate these jobs. Through proper planning and staffing, a manager should know which employees have the time to do the work. Delegating work, particularly routine clerical work, to others is a management function. If the supervisor firmly believes in this principle and has the desire, delegating this work will not be difficult. Once a manager overcomes inertia and begins the delegation process, it becomes a way of life and all future clerical assignments that flow into the manager's department are dispersed immediately to the employees. This is getting work done through other people.

Many minor decisions can be delegated back to the employees requesting the decision. Most of these decisions are associated with a dollar amount, and the quantity of minor decisions can be greatly reduced by giving employees the responsibility for making their own decisions up to a certain dollar limit. Tellers, for example, can be given authority to cash certain checks up to specified dollar amounts without seeking managerial approval. Customer service personnel can be permitted to rebate or waive overdraft charges, checkbook charges, and other bank service charges within defined limits. Minor staffing problems such as employee requests to switch their days off or planned vacation times can be solved by requesting that the employees find other employees with whom to trade.

Routine questions asked by an employee about the way to handle a particular transaction can often be answered by the employee if the manager takes the time to make the employee think for himeslf. Turning the questions back onto the employee with questions like "What did you do the last time this happened?" or "How do *you* think this should be handled?" will help to train the employee to think for himself and eventually will lead to fewer questions being asked. This same procedure can be used when employees are relaying simple questions asked by customers. Many employees, if given an easy choice, will tend to run to the manager with every question posed to them. They use the manager as a mental crutch. By not giving an immediate response to these questions but rather by forcing employees to use their own knowledge to answer questions, the supervisor is saving his time and is training employees to be more independent and more valuable to themselves and the bank.

In larger departments, senior clerks, assistant managers, and the like can be trained to answer more difficult questions, to make more important decisions, and even to perform certain daily management functions like the routine staffing and scheduling of employees.

Delegation, therefore, is an important organizational tool. It expands the amount of important work that a manager can accomplish because it is a time-saving function. It provides a faster flow of work through a department by eliminating the bottleneck of all things having to be approved, decided, or answered by the manager. It provides employees with opportunities to assume more responsibility, to gain in experience, to expand their interests, and to increase their motivation.

IV

Decision Making

Decision making is a function that is used in all areas of management, especially in planning, scheduling, staffing, and delegating. Decision making is developing the correct course of action for the solution of a problem. There are four parts to this function: Know the problem, research solutions, act, and follow up.

Know the Problem

Putting a label on the problem such as "poor employee morale" is not knowing the problem. It is merely categorizing it. It is important to know the cause or causes of the problem. What is causing poor morale?—haphazard scheduling, unfair management policies, uneven work assignments, inadequate training? Without knowing the causes, solutions cannot be developed. The causes of a problem can be determined through observation, by asking questions of others in the department (particularly the more experienced employees), and by consulting with higher management. The manager's manager probably has had more experience in management and banking than the manager and can often offer a list of stock causes for a specific problem. For example, if the problem is excessive check-cashing losses in the teller area, then the list of potential causes might be: poor teller training, lack of definitive check-cashing guidelines, the inaccessibility of records (signature cards, and trial balances), and/or not enough supervisors available for check approvals. From this list a manager can select those causes that he feels pertain most directly to the particular situation.

How big a problem is it? How big is the decision going to be? This is determined by the cost to the bank in either loss of revenue or increased expense, and the effect on the employees in the department. These are the criteria upon which the manager measures the size of a problem. The bigger the problem, the more time will be required to determine its causes and eventual solutions. A decision regarding the approval of a check for cashing, for example, can be big or small depending on the dollar amount of the check—the potential financial loss to the bank.

Research Solutions

Once the causes of the problem have been identified, the task of developing solutions begins. Developing solutions to any problem requires research. The bigger the problem, the more important research becomes. Researching solutions involves drawing upon the manager's own experience and the experience of others, peers and supervisors, who have solved similar problems. The experiences of bankers in other banks are often overlooked as sources of solutions to problems in management. Bankers are often willing to be of help to one another. Very few problems are original. There are thousands of banks in the country and the managers in these banks are all experiencing the same problems. The probability is great that someone somewhere has already solved your problems. Consequently, developing good relationships with other bankers is important. Correspondent banks particularly will often help. Trade publications often publish articles outlining solutions to specific problems which are common to many banks.

All problems have solutions. Some problems have many solutions. If the research has been adequate, a list of potential solutions will have been developed. To this list imagination has to be applied. Parts of one solution can be used with parts of others. Solutions can be rearranged by adding to them, subtracting from them, and reversing them. Advantages and disadvantages of potential solutions must be recognized before they can be properly evaluated. Only after all known solutions have been evaluated can a manager make a decision—choosing the best solution for the problem. As a precautionary measure, it is advisable to wait at least twenty-four hours before acting on a decision. This will allow the decision to "age" and possibly avoid action on an impractical solution.

Act

The most important part of the decision-making process is acting upon the accepted solution. The solution may be the best thought-out, most ingenious one ever devised by man, but it has no value unless it is acted upon. Major problems always require action. No action at all with regard to a major problem is often worse than acting with the wrong solution. Action will instigate more action. Even if the solution has had some previously unthought of disadvantages, these can be corrected during implementation. The key point is to ACT.

The timeliness of the action to be taken is an important consideration. Acting too quickly or too slowly can often seriously influence the effectiveness of a decision. For example, if the solution for solving a temporary backlog of work in the department is to ask everyone in the department to work overtime on one night next week, don't wait until that night to ask them. That is acting too slowly. Give the employees enough time to plan to work the extra hours. Conversely, if a decision has been made to promote one of the employees within the department to a position which will not be available for three months, don't tell the employee about it now. That is acting too quickly. Something might happen during the three month period that would alter the circumstances and force a reevaluation of the decision to promote the employee.

Follow-up

All major decisions put into action require follow-up by the manager to be certain that the solution has been put into action on a consistent basis as originally planned. In addition, the best of solutions usually requires some adjustments. The follow-up process provides the manager with the opportunity to assess the plan in action and make adjustments as needed.

A Study in Decision Making

The following study incorporates not only the four parts of the decision-making process, but it also includes elements of planning, delegating, and operating within an organized structure.

One day, Donald Schwartz, vice president in charge of the branch administration division, was reviewing the monthly operating reports of the three branches in his division. Suddenly he became alarmed upon noticing a marked increase in operating losses at the South Branch during the past month. In fact, although all three branches were approximately the same size, the South Branch showed operating losses over four times the amount in each of the other two branches.

At this point, Mr. Schwartz knew that a loss problem existed in the South Branch. He was able to label the problem as "excessive losses" but he didn't really know what was causing the problem. Therefore, he immediately took the following steps to further identify the problem and its causes.

To obtain a broader picture of the problem he quickly reviewed his monthly reports on operating losses for the South Branch for the past twelve months and he found that only during the past month had the operating losses increased dramatically. Then Mr. Schwartz, correctly following the organizational chain of command, telephoned Robert Mott, the manager of the South Branch, to investigate the situation. Mr. Mott informed Mr. Schwartz that the large increase in losses during the previous month was due to a number of bad checks that were cashed by the tellers during that month. Mr. Schwartz then suggested he meet with Mr. Mott at the South Branch the next morning to investigate the problem further, and he requested that all records pertaining to the previous month's check losses be available at the meeting. Mr. Mott then suggested that the teller supervisor of the branch be invited to the meeting as a help in investigating the check loss problem.

At nine o'clock on the following morning all three levels of management in the branch administration division (Division Manager Schwartz, Branch Manager Mott, and the manager of the teller department) met in Mott's office. The three managers then proceeded to learn about the problem (step one in the decision-making process). Mr. Mott presented the bad checks that were cashed during the previous month. There were eleven checks. The managers proceeded to analyze and compare the checks to determine a common denominator for the problem by listing all the facts about each check taken in chronological order by date of cashing. Figure 5 shows this list. Mr. Mott then stated that the three smaller checks that were drawn on their bank caused overdrafts that the bank was unable to collect. This type of problem, he noted, was not uncommon in the branch for a typical month. The obvious bad check problem, Mr. Mott deducted, was with the other eight checks which were all returned by the drawee banks for the reason "account closed." All were supposedly endorsed by good long-standing customers of the bank (Forbes, Inland and Stokes). When the checks were charged back to these customers' accounts, however, all three claimed that they never saw the checks before and never presented them to a teller for cashing. Upon reviewing the endorsements on these checks with the signature cards signed by these customers, they found that the signatures looked genuine. Furthermore, Mr. Mott stated that the person or persons presenting these checks had put the correct account number of the customer on the back of each check to further aid the teller in identification.

By this time, it was obvious to all three managers that on April 13, 14, and 15 the branch was invaded by one or more bad-check passers who had assumed the identities of reputable

Figure 5

April Bad Check Problem—South Branch

Date Cashed	Teller	Amount of check	Maker	Payee	Endorser	Drawee Bank
4/4	M. Tevlas	$ 17.00	R. Raymond	R. Raymond	R. Raymond	On Us
4/13	S. Erhardt	265.00	Able Constr. Co.	D. Forbes	D. Forbes	ABC Bank
4/13	F. Tevlas	325.00	R&S Bakery	L. Stokes	L. Stokes	XYZ Bank
4/14	T. Holmes	50.00	W. Mason	W. Mason	W. Mason	On Us
4/14	F. Cohen	245.00	Easy Repair Co.	G. Inland	G. Inland	BCD Bank
4/14	C. Kittle	295.00	Easy Repair Co.	G. Inland	G. Inland	BCD Bank
4/14	C. Kittle	310.00	Able Constr. Co.	G. Inland	G. Inland	ABC Bank
4/15	T. Holmes	235.00	R&S Bakery	L. Stokes	L. Stokes	XYZ Bank
4/15	T. Holmes	305.00	Able Constr. Co.	D. Forbes	D. Forbes	ABC Bank
4/15	F. Cohen	300.00	R&S Bakery	L. Stokes	L. Stokes	XYZ Bank
4/28	S. Rafferty	12.00	J. Andrews	J. Andrews	J. Andrews	On Us

customers and proceeded to present to the bank, for cashing, checks that were drawn on closed accounts. Somehow, probably by illegally tampering with the mails, they temporarily obtained these customers' checking account statements. These statements provided the check passers with sufficient information (copies of signatures from cancelled checks, account numbers, and balances) about the legitimate customer to pose as the real customer.

The three managers continued to compare the facts shown on their list of bad checks (figure 5). Only the eight large checks were analyzed. At first, there appeared to be no common denominator. Several tellers were involved. Three different checks were used. Three different customers' names were used, and the checks were presented on three different dates. Further examination, however, did reveal two important facts. All the checks were drawn on other banks (Not On Us), and the checks ranged in amounts between $200 and $350.

Up to this point the three managers were learning about the problem. The problem could now be properly defined as a loss problem caused by the cashing of a series of checks over a three day period which were all drawn on other banks, ranging in amounts between $200 and $350. These checks were presented by persons who assumed the identity of good, financially responsible customers of the bank. Because of the total loss to the bank of $2280, the problem of how to eliminate this problem in the future had to be solved immediately.

Step two in the decision-making process, researching solutions, could now begin. By this time it was lunch hour and Mr. Mott, the branch manager, had a luncheon appointment with an important customer of the branch and suggested to Mr. Schwartz that he might wish to join them. While they were at lunch, Mr. Mott delegated the responsibility to the teller department manager of calling two or three of the other banks in the area to determine how they may have solved a similar check-cashing problem. It was then agreed that they would all meet again in Mr. Mott's office at 2:00 P.M. to develop and decide upon a solution to the problem.

At 2:00 P.M. all three managers reassembled in Mr. Mott's office. The manager of the teller department reported that he was able to contact three other banks in the area; two of the banks had cashed two checks each during April and these checks were cashed under the same circumstances as the eight checks in the South Branch. Since the losses in each of the other banks, however, totaled less than $500, the other banks were not as alarmed about the incidents and had not yet established any additional procedures to protect themselves from this type of loss. They merely enforced their present procedures with the tellers involved, but admitted that this was not adequate.

Mr. Schwartz then stated that the calls to the other banks had at least confirmed the way these bad-check passers operated, and he proceeded to write down an outline of their method of operation.

1. Checks are in amounts of $200 or more.
2. Checks are always drawn on another bank.
3. Check passer assumes identity of a legitimate customer by presenting the check to the teller already endorsed with a reasonably good facsimile of the customer's handwriting; often on the back of the check the customer's account number is written above or underneath the endorsement.

Mr. Schwartz then suggested that the three of them join in a brainstorming session as the first step in developing a solution to the problem. He said that in a brainstorming session all suggestions, ideas, and comments, regardless of their merit, are acceptable and not to be criticized. All contributions, however, should be related to the solving of the problem. Mr. Mott agreed to write down all the comments. At the end of about an hour of brainstorming, Mr. Mott had eighteen ideas, comments and suggestions listed as follows.

1. Have a manager approve all checks before they are cashed.

2. Have a manager approve all Not On Us checks before they are cashed.
3. Provide a picture identification card for all customers.
4. Don't trust signatures as a form of identification.
5. Don't consider the knowledge of an account number as identification.
6. Knowledge of mother's maiden name is a good form of identification.
7. Possession of pre-printed checks and deposits is a form of identification.
8. Fingerprint all customers.
9. Take pictures of all customers cashing checks.
10. Train tellers in how check passers operate.
11. Teach tellers how to identify customers.
12. Have a manager approve all Not On Us checks over $200 presented for cashing.
13. Use drivers license as identification.
14. Call drawee bank before cashing Not On Us checks.
15. Have customer endorse check in front of teller.
16. Use possession of a savings passbook as a form of identification.
17. If check is already endorsed when presented, have customer endorse check again while covering up first endorsement, or have him endorse the check on the other end in such a way that first endorsement appears upside down, thereby making it more difficult to copy.
18. Teach tellers that to know a customer means to be able to identify the face with a name and not just to recognize a familiar face.

From this list the managers proceeded to organize the suggestions into categories and to sort out those that seemed too impractical to adopt. The eighteen suggestions were sorted into two main categories.

1. Check approval ideas.
2. Ways of identifying customers.

The suggestions regarding customer picture identification cards, fingerprinting customers, and taking pictures of customers cashing checks were ruled out because of the logistic problems, inconvenience to customers, and the expense involved in adopting these systems. Next, the more general ideas such as "have a manager approve all checks before they are cashed" and "teach tellers how to identify customers" were combined with the specific ideas concerning these subjects. Much consideration was given to requiring that someone in management approve all checks over $200 drawn on other banks. Because of the number of checks of this kind being presented each day, however, more managers would have to be hired to service the tellers. It was decided, therefore, that the tellers would continue to determine whether or not to cash these checks, but that they would be better trained in identification procedures. Most importantly, tellers would be required to learn a stricter, more detailed identification procedure than the traditional one of comparing endorsement signatures to signatures filed at the bank. This new identification procedure would be required on all checks presented for cashing that were $200 or more and not drawn on the bank. The following outline of this procedure was developed.

Teller Identification Procedure
for Cashing Not On Us Checks
of $200 or More

If the teller cannot positively identify the customer (the face with the name) on sight, the following identification procedure is required.

Identify the customer by requesting a driver's license and comparing the signature on the license with the endorsement that was signed in front of the teller.

OR

Any *two* of the following forms of identification will be required:

1. Compare the endorsement signature signed in front of teller to the bank's signature card file.

2. Compare the customer's mother's maiden name with the bank's record of this information as noted on the signature card.

3. Note the customer's possession, perhaps in conjunction with another transaction, of a pre-printed checking-account deposit slip or check, or a savings passbook showing the customer's name.

Any other forms of identification should be referred to the manager for approval before the check is cashed.

Now that the solution of the problem had been decided upon, the next step was to *act*. Because of the recent large losses involved, it was decided to act immediately. The same afternoon plans were made to type the new identification procedure and present it to the tellers in a meeting to be scheduled the following afternoon. At the meeting it was planned to inform all the tellers about the check losses, show them the checks that were cashed, explain the check passers' method of operation, and introduce the new identification procedure. Mr. Schwartz delegated the responsibility of conducting the teller meeting and introducing the new procedures to Mr. Mott, the branch manager, who in turn delegated to the teller manager the responsibility of notifying the tellers of the meeting, making sure they were all present, and preparing the necessary written materials.

By this time it was four o'clock in the afternoon and it was time for Mr. Schwartz to return to the main bank. Before leaving, however, he suggested that their decision, after it was in effect for two weeks, be evaluated for any changes that might be required (follow-up), and that the three of them meet two weeks from that day to discuss any problems that may have developed with the new procedure.

Two weeks later when the managers had their follow-up meeting, the teller manager reported that the new procedure was understood by the tellers and in use without exception, but that the tellers were encountering adverse reaction from the customers. Some customers, particularly those who had been customers of the bank for years, were annoyed upon being asked for additional forms of identification and/or to endorse the check again in front of the teller. This follow-up information presented a new problem to be solved. But by again following the four decision-making steps, this problem was eventually solved. The bank developed a small campaign to educate check-cashing customers about the need for these precautionary procedures.

V
Training and Developing Employees

In all the words written and spoken about the functions of management and getting things done through other people, too little emphasis is placed on the training and developing of those people who are to get the things done. Managers, of course, have to be communicators. They have to be motivators. They have to be organizers. Just as important, they have to be, at least in a broad sense, teachers. Even though they may not directly train new employees in specific skills, managers must direct the activities of those who do the training. Types of training have to be decided upon. Subject matter and method of presentation have to be determined. The trainer has to be carefully selected. Then, when each employee has mastered the basic skills required to perform the job, the manager's more direct function of developing each employee to his potential within the bank begins. The management function of training and developing employees has a mutually beneficial effect for the manager, the employees, and the bank. The manager will get the job done better, thus reflecting upon his own accomplishments. Employees will be motivated to do better work in their present jobs, and that in turn will lead them to more important jobs in the department and the bank. The bank will prosper and grow because of the correctly channeled efforts of the employees. And as the bank grows, all employees will have the opportunity to grow into the new and expanding departments that will result.

Training

Training refers to the teaching of necessary concepts and skills to employees in such a way as to enable them to perform their jobs to the best of their ability. These concepts and skills include knowledge of how the department and the bank functions, how to perform each clerical function of a particular job, how to operate any business machine required (adding machine, teller machine, typewriter, dictaphone, proof machine, film machine, copying machine, etc.), and in many bank jobs, how to serve customers correctly.

In order to teach people concepts and skills, those responsible for training must know the basic principles involved in the learning process. Only through an understanding of these principles can an effective program for training be developed. The four basic principles in the learning process are: the learner's desire (motivation) to learn the job, the effective presentation of the duties of the job, practice, and evaluation. The absence of any one of these conditions will either completely block or seriously hinder the learning process.

An obvious prerequisite to the learning process should be mentioned here—the ability of an employee to learn a special job. Determining the ability of a person to learn a job was discussed in chapter 2 in the section on interviewing job applicants. If a person does not have the correct personality or proficiency for a job, only parts of the job will be learned at best. The whole job will never be learned to a degree acceptable to management. Accordingly, to attempt to train the employee would be largely a wasted effort.

Motivation to Learn

The motivation or desire to learn a specific job is an essential condition of the learning process. This desire predisposes the learner's mind to accept eagerly the information to be learned. Conversely, without this desire a mental block is created in the learner's mind which will not permit new information to be received. Human beings are motivated to learn and do things because they perceive these things as good for themselves in some way. New employees are usually excited about starting a new job, and they are naturally motivated to learn. This initial motivation, though often sound at the outset, is frail. If not constantly fortified through the learning process, it could easily disintegrate. Reinforcement of the motivation to learn is required all during the learning process as will be seen when the other principles of learning are discussed. The subject of motivation is more fully discussed in the next chapter. But it is important to note here that motivation is required for the learning process to be successful.

Effective Presentation of the Subject

Effective presentation of the subject is the core of the learning process. In most managers' minds this is training. Effective presentation of the duties and skills of the job is a communications effort. It is the transmission of knowledge from one person to another in such a way as to be fully understood by the recipient. The following points will be helpful in effectively communicating new job duties to trainees. All these points relate to training employees in any new job assignments. To provide continuity throughout this presentation, however, the examples given relate to the training of bank tellers, which is often the biggest clerical training job in most banks.

Make no assumptions. Those employees who have the responsibility of training others often make assumptions with regard to the amount of knowledge already possessed by the trainee. It may often be assumed, for example, that teller trainees have a basic understanding of checks, deposits, checking accounts, and savings accounts because they have had direct personal experience with these fundamental subjects. Surprisingly, most trainees, regardless of their age or non-business background, have very little knowledge about these basic terms and bank services. Even the knowledge new employees have acquired in previous bank work experience about teller work should be suspect until proven otherwise.

The trainer should make no assumptions when using specific banking terms. All bank or business-related words should be defined by the trainer as they are being used. The trainer, who is an experienced bank employee, has developed a vocabulary of banking terms which through constant daily use has become an automatic way of speaking. Bank words such as tape, rags, strap, fiche, cashier's check, hold, money order, cash in, cash out, coupon, blotter, and the like are common words for the experienced teller. They are often foreign words to the trainee.

Organize the subject matter. Much is accomplished with organization; the human mind will grasp concepts presented in an orderly way. And so the subject matter must be divided into its basic parts. Each basic part is then divided into sub-parts and taught to the trainee. This takes planning before the trainee arrives in the department. And this planning is the responsibility of the department supervisor. The supervisor should take an active role in organizing the subject to be certain that all parts of the subject are covered with the trainee. In many banks one person may not be training all trainees. The training work could be divided among many. A written detailed outline of the subject, prepared by the supervisor, will greatly reduce the possibility of a particular trainer neglecting to present to the trainee a vital part of the job.

Figure 6 shows a typical detailed outline of the subject matter to be covered when training a universal teller. The subject matter is divided into nine major parts. This outline begins with an orientation section which is an important part of training any employee in any new job. Many banks have general orientation sessions for all new employees which cover a brief history of the bank, its personnel policies, and its banking facilities and services. Few department managers, however, consider developing their own orientation program which explains to the employee the role of the department within the bank, the various activities that go on in that department, and how the particular job to be learned fits into the overall function of the department. New universal-teller trainees, for example, should be oriented toward the importance of their job as they are often the only contact the customer has with the bank. They should know that the deposits received through the teller window become the money that the bank uses to loan out to other customers for interest income—the major source of income for the bank. They should realize that a bank grows in direct proportion to the amount of these deposits. This shows the teller trainee how important the teller function is in the overall picture. Also, the teller trainee should be given a tour, with accompanying explanation, of the various sections of the teller department to show the scope of the departmental functions. An orientation session such as this provides the trainee with further interest and additional motivation to learn about this new job which is vital to the overall well-being of the bank.

The eight remaining sections are arranged in a logical sequence starting with the simple (cash handling, cash security, teller machine operation, processing deposits) and leading to the complex (processing withdrawals, balancing procedure). The subjects should also be arranged so that the most frequent basic activities performed in the job are taught first (cash handling, processing deposits and withdrawals, balancing) and other activities (processing other transactions) second. The variety of these transactions tend to confuse the trainee if presented earlier in the program. The trainee should not be deluged with too many new concepts during the first stages of the program. Even within each major part of the outline the principle of starting with the simple and leading to the complex should be considered. The trainee must learn, for example, about the parts of a check before being taught the clearance of checks, and he should learn the clearance of checks before being introduced to the concept of uncollected funds. Starting with the complex will merely frustrate the learner, demotivate him, and inhibit his perception of the subject.

Once the basic skills of the job have been absorbed, the important concept of customer service should be introduced. Not only in teller work but in many bank positions, this is an important subject. A bank is a retail business and it depends on its customers for survival and growth.

The section on interdepartmental relationships is designed to show the trainee how the teller department directly relates to

Figure 6
Universal Teller Training Program

I. ORIENTATION

   A. Introduce New Employee to Other Employees
   B. Tour of Department
      1. Explain department's function within bank
      2. Explain each section's function within department
   C. Review Departmental Personnel Policies
   D. Brief Introduction to the Importance of Good Customer Service

II. CASH HANDLING AND SECURITY

   A. Handling Coin and Currency
      1. Counting
      2. Packaging
      3. Ordering
      4. Transferring
      5. Mutilated money
      6. Foreign money
      7. Cash ins and cash outs
   B. Cash Security
      1. Alarm and camera systems
      2. Bait money
      3. Hold up procedures
      4. Counterfeit money
      5. Swindle schemes
      6. Vault procedures

III. PROCESSING DEPOSITS

   A. Teller Machine Operation
   B. Receiving Deposits
      1. Checking
      2. Savings
      3. Straight (no cash back) deposits
      4. Split (cash back) deposits
      5. Customer receipts
      6. Night deposits
      7. Mail deposits
      8. No passbook deposits
      9. Savings account interest
     10. Posting interest

IV. PROCESSING WITHDRAWALS

   A. Savings Withdrawals
      1. Signature verification
      2. Balance verification
      3. Approval limits
   B. Check Cashing
      1. Explanation of check—parts, clearance, types, uncollected funds
      2. Verification procedure— dates, alterations, sufficient balance, signature, stops, holds, endorsements
      3. Approval limits
      4. Fraudulent check cashing schemes

V. BALANCING PROCEDURE

A. Debit-Credit Principle
B. Balancing Principle
C. Teller's Blotter

D. Finding Differences
E. Teller Difference
   Guidelines

VI. PROCESSING OTHER TRANSACTIONS

A. Money Orders
B. Drafts
C. Cashiers Checks
D. Certified Checks
E. Savings Bonds

F. Traveler's Checks
G. Christmas Clubs
H. Utility Payments
I. Loan Payments
J. Property Taxes

VIII. CUSTOMER SERVICE

A. Importance of the
   Customer
B. Teller Attitude
C. Friendliness
   1. Greeting customers
   2. Thanking customers
D. Personal Appearance
E. Accuracy
F. Neatness

G. Confidentiality
H. Handling customer
   situations
   1. Officer referrals
   2. Identification
   3. Customer lines
   4. Mistakes
   5. Irate Customers

VIII. INTERDEPARTMENTAL RELATIONSHIPS

A. Proof and Transit Department
B. Bookkeeping Department
C. Savings Department

D. Personal Banking Department
E. Computer Center
F. Collection Department

IX. OTHER BANK SERVICES

A. Certificates of Deposits
B. Safe Deposit Boxes
C. Notary Public
D. New Accounts

E. Loan Services
F. Trust Services
G. Wire Transfers
H. Banking Hours

certain other departments of the bank. It is important that the trainee know the flow of work—where it comes from and where it goes—how these departments depend on one another, and how the quality of work done by employees in one department effects employees in other departments. This overall knowledge will help motivate the trainee to do higher quality work.

The last section of this outline—other bank services —presents a subject which is often neglected in the training of bank employees. Although of obvious value to tellers, this subject is valuable to all bank employees. Employees should have at least an awareness of what other services the bank offers besides those directly offered in the department where the employee works. In most training programs time is a critical factor, and to present this subject in detail is often not practical. If the employee at least knows what these services are and where they are offered, it will be helpful to the employee in dealing with customers or when talking to friends outside the bank. It makes the employee feel part of something larger, and it may motivate him in the future to educate himself further.

If a written outline of the training program similar to the one shown in figure 6 is given to the trainee at the beginning of his training, the trainee knows from the start and all during the program what is expected of him in terms of the subjects he is required to learn. The outline serves as a knowledge goal for the trainee and will help him to organize in his own mind the job to be learned.

Present the subject. Psychologists and educators agree that a person learns faster and retains longer that which is perceived through several senses. The learning process is primarily centered around three of the five human senses—hearing, seeing, and touching. Of these three senses seeing is the most powerful; but even more powerful is learning through all three senses in combination. Thus, when teaching a teller trainee the way to count money, it is best that the trainee not only hear the explanation but see and handle money during the same training session. Likewise, when taught about checks, the trainee should hear the explanations and see and be permitted to touch sample checks. The samples of money, checks, deposit slips, savings withdrawal slips, passbooks, etc. should be as close to the real thing as possible. Real transactions that have been prepared by customers are better than mock transactions. The closer the training tools are to the reality, the better prepared the trainee will be. Trainees are better versed in the use of banking forms if they are permitted to practice with "live" work received through the night depository, the mail, and armored carrier deliveries.

The old adage "a picture is worth a thousand words" is true as it relates to the learning process. Visual perception is very powerful. The use of visual aids in teaching has long been recognized for its importance. In these times the use of the more glamorous visual aids such as television, movies, and color slides or film strips immediately comes to mind. Unfortunately, some banking subjects have not been produced on these mediums, or if available, are too expensive for most banks' budgets. The less glamorous but often equally effective visual aids such as the blackboard, flip chart, or opaque projector (a machine that projects onto a screen anything that is written or printed on a flat opaque surface) are easily within every bank's budget. Even a drawing, chart, or graph produced on paper and duplicated and distributed to the trainee is an effective visual aid. With any visual aid, an explanation of what is being viewed is essential. This explanation can be given either by the trainer live or by a voice on a sound track, cassette tape, or phonograph record.

An often overlooked type of visual aid is the written word. Typewritten sheets or books on a particular subject offer an excellent vehicle for training. An explanation of a subject in prose form permits the trainee to study the material on his own at his own pace. The trainee also can form questions for later discussion. This same written material can be used again and again to refresh a trainee's memory on a particular point. The written word is of special use in teaching concepts such as the clearance of checks, uncollected funds, fraudulent check-cashing schemes, float, balancing, debit-credit principle, and the like. These concepts require study and cannot be learned in a quick oral lesson. Managers and trainers should investigate sources of already prepared audio and visual aids that are available from the American Bankers Association, the Bank Administration Institute, and the various publishing firms that specialize in banking subjects.

The trainee should be shown how to do the job correctly in detail from the beginning. Haphazard, vague, incomplete teaching of skills will only lead the trainee immediately into poor habits which are difficult to correct.

A lesson can be learned from the way subject matter is presented in fifty-minute time segments in primary, secondary, and college level schools. It is amazing how the human mind can absorb the subject of mathematics the first hour of the day, a foreign language next, followed by history, English, chemistry, and so on throughout the day. The mind is actually refreshed by the change of subject matter and can absorb information about different subjects hour after hour. On the other hand, being taught one subject for several hours produces disinterest, boredom, and lack of concentration. When training employees, therefore, introduce several different subjects each day in fifty to sixty-minute time periods. This is not only possible but also highly recommended.

Part of teaching a subject is to permit and encourage two-way communication between the trainer and the trainee. Trainees should be allowed to ask questions and discuss the subject being presented. No matter how elementary the question may seem, the trainer should not criticize the question but rather answer it patiently. The answer might be key information to the trainee. It might produce a complete understanding of a concept for the trainee. Two-way communication in the teaching process not only accelerates comprehension, but it also indicates to the trainer the extent to which the subject is being comprehended.

In summary, the subject is better learned by the trainee if it is presented in accordance with the following general principles:

1. Make no assumptions about the trainee's knowledge.
2. Prepare a detailed, logically-organized written outline of the subject to be covered and give it to the trainee.
3. Start with the simple and lead into the complex.

4. Teach the basic concepts first.
5. Whenever possible, teach in a way which involves the senses of seeing, hearing, and touching.
6. Use "real" objects whenever practical.
7. Use visual aids extensively.
8. Present concepts through the written word.
9. Teach skills correctly and in detail from the beginning.
10. Change subject matter frequently during the day.
11. Encourage questions and discussion.

Practice

Another basic element of the learning process is practice. Practice is that part of the learning process which impresses the subject matter on a person's mind in such a way that it can be easily recalled from memory. No matter how well the subject is explained and understood, without practice the mind will eventually lose its ability to recall it from memory instantaneously and in its complete form. A subject is not learned, therefore, until first it is presented to and understood by the learner, and then remembered. Practice helps the learner to remember. In the academic world practice takes the form of study, memorization, and review when studying for tests and final examinations. In the business world practice takes the form of applying concepts that have been explained and understood, such as uncollected funds, business-account service charge analysis, and methods of computing savings-account interest. Practice involves applying them repeatedly in real banking situations or performing repeatedly physical actions such as counting money, operating teller machines, and processing transactions.

Learning a subject completely means not only understanding the subject, but also being able to recall this understanding from memory at any time in the future. Regardless of whether the matter to be recalled from memory is conceptual (the definition of uncollected funds) or a skill (counting money), only practice will etch the concept or skill into memory. Without practice only fragmented knowledge about the subject will be retained at best and the subject matter cannot be considered to be fully assimilated.

Following are some general principles about the subject of practice that should be kept in mind by those who engage in the training of others.

Concepts can be practiced. The process by which checking and savings-account balances can be considered uncollected is a subject which can be practiced. A teller, for example, can retrace in his mind this concept each time he cashes a check or processes a savings account withdrawal. By repeatedly applying the principle to a work situation, he is practicing the principle. At first the mental process involved is difficult. The mind is groping to remember the principle. Parts of the principle which may apply to a particular situation may have already been temporarily forgotten, thus the teller will require a quick review from someone or from some written material during an idle moment. Slowly, however, with practice, the groping is reduced until finally the mind can instantly recall the principle at will.

Practice promotes more complete understanding of concepts. Applying a subject that has been explained to real situations solidifies and better organizes the subject matter in the trainee's mind. And in this way, any points about the subject which may not have been mentioned or fully explained will become evident. Investigating these points will lead to a broader and richer understanding of the subject matter. The trainer cannot possibly provide an exhaustive coverage of the subject during the explanation period; enrichment comes from repeated practice.

The practice of skills promotes speed in performing these skills. The bank clerical skills of filing, sorting, counting, typing, operating machines, etc. require practice in order to promote speed. These skills require physical activity which the trainee is not used to performing. Muscles and senses have to become acclimated and coordinated to the new activity. Accuracy cannot be sacrificed for speed. During the beginning stages of practice, accuracy and the correct way of performing the job must be emphasized continually. To allow a trainee to perform a skill incorrectly for any period of time will encourage the immediate formation of bad habits which will be difficult, if not impossible, to correct in the future. After the correct procedure has been learned, speed can be emphasized. During the early stages of practice generous amounts of encouragement and praise are required to motivate the trainee with the desire to continue with training. This encouragement and praise will also counteract the frustration that often exists when a person learns a new skill. Frustration inhibits learning.

Although all trainees may be given the same amount of practice time to acquire skills, they will acquire skills at different rates of speed. Each person is different. Many will acquire skills somewhere within prescribed time frames. Others may learn faster or slower. Allowances should be made for those who do not learn certain skills according to schedule.

Short practice sessions of a particular skill are more effective than long sessions. This is particularly true in the beginning stages of practice. A new teller trainee, for example, usually starts skill practice by counting money. But to allow a new trainee just to count money hour after hour is ineffective. It is better to confine this practice to half-hour segments with perhaps an hour break in between. During these breaks, another skill can be practiced, or another concept can be explained.

Practicing skills in combination is effective. This introduces the building-block principle in training. Teller positions, like many banking jobs, require learning many skills and concepts. The basic skills of the teller's job (counting money, operating teller machines, processing transactions, etc.) should be taught one at a time but in rapid succession. On the first training day, for example, after basic orientation concerning the teller job, the trainee should receive an explanation of the correct way to count money. Practice can then follow closely (during the same day) with an explanation and practice of the teller's machine. Examples of the basic types of items processed by a teller can be used. The second day's practice session would also include the counting of money and the use of the teller machines using the same types of transactions. New types of transactions are now explained and added to the practice session. Each day all things practiced on previous days are again practiced. The only change is that new concepts and skills are added each day and practiced along with the old skills. This process continues throughout the duration of the training program.

Goal setting is a vital element of practice. Trainees are better motivated to perform well as a result of practice if they know what is expected of them. Trainees should be shown an outline of the training program which shows the projected number of days allowed for each part of the program to be learned. This will motivate the employee to "learn on schedule" to the best of his ability. Later on during the training, other goals regarding what is expected of trained tellers when they are on the job should be introduced. Performance standards such as "Teller differences should be limited to no more than X number per month and no more than X dollars in accumulated shortages per month" are goals which promote accuracy. Without goals, people will perform aimlessly or develop their own goals which in no way relate to those considered appropriate by management.

Practice promotes recall from memory. It is a well-known phenomenon that people who in their youth learned and practiced for a long period of time certain types of physical activity such as riding a bicycle, swimming, and driving a car, or business-related activities such as typing and operating an adding or key punch machine, can, after years of inactivity, recall these skills from memory. What may not be so obvious is that this same phenomenon occurs with conceptual subject matter. The concept of uncollected funds, for example, if applied over and over again to beyond the point where it has just been understood, can be so etched into memory that, even after a long period of disuse, it can be recalled. No one can define exactly how long a period of practice is required in the beginning to enable a person to recall a concept from memory after a long period of disuse. What is known, however, is that, in the beginning, this practice period must be much longer than what is required only to understand the subject completely. Unfortunately, forgetting begins soon after learning has been completed. Practice will retard this forgetting process, and often it will permit recall many years after the material has not been consciously used.

Evaluation

The last basic element of the learning process is evaluation or testing. Throughout the entire training program, the trainer should be constantly evaluating the trainee's progress. If simple questioning determines that certain concepts are not fully understood, then these concepts should be explained again and discussed until the trainee understands. If observation determines that certain skills are not being learned, then more concentrated practice may be required. Trainees can easily deceive a trainer about what he has learned. Questions like "Do you understand?" or "Is there anything you don't understand?" are not enough. Direct questions like "Explain the debit-credit principle" or "What is the first thing you do when you're out of balance?" are required. The trainee cannot escape revealing his possible lack of knowledge when asked these questions. A series of key questions about each concept should be devised and used throughout the training after these concepts have been explained and studied by the trainee. The process of direct questioning, whether in written or oral form, provides strong motivation for the trainee to listen and try to understand concepts rather than let his mind wander during the explanation process. The trainer, to use this technique properly as a motivator, should mention to the trainee at the beginning of the program that direct questioning will be used throughout as an aid to the learning process.

There is nothing revolutionary about the questioning process. Schools have been using it for centuries through quizzes, tests, and written and oral examinations. It is still the only effective way to determine if a person has learned what has been taught.

In addition to using questions throughout training, time can be set aside halfway through and/or at the end of the training period for administering a more formal and comprehensive oral or written test. Oral tests are better than written tests because they allow questions and answers to be explained and clarified on the spot. The disadvantage of oral testing is that the test can only be given to one trainee at a time; written tests are more practical with a group that is being trained together.

The Trainer

Each year banks throughout the country train thousands of first-level clerical employees. The majority of banks use the "buddy system." A few banks have developed formalized programs, particularly in the teller area. Regardless of what system a bank may use, the effectiveness of any training program depends not only on the way the subject is presented, but also on the competency of the person doing the training. The trainer must know the subject matter and be willing and able to effectively communicate the subject to the trainee. To be competent, the trainer must possess the following qualifications.

Knowledge of the subject. One cannot teach what one does not know. In choosing a trainer, remember that the fastest or most senior employee is not necessarily the most knowledgeable. What is important is the scope of the trainer's understanding of the subject. Trainees should be encouraged to ask a lot of questions, and the trainer should know the answers. A knowledgeable trainer will gain the confidence of the trainee at the beginning and will always be in command of the training situation.

Ability to communicate the subject effectively. Teaching a subject requires most of all that the trainer know and use the techniques already described in this chapter and in chapter 2 (communicating). In addition, the trainer should be willing to devise or acquire, and use, visual and audio aids.

Personal qualifications. A list of many personal qualifications could be devised that would be the ideal. Of special importance, however, is that the trainer be mature, patient, enthusiastic, and imaginative. Maturity insures that the trainer will understand and get along with the various types of people to be trained. Patience is a virtue that is needed in abundance because the untrained with their initial clumsiness, lack of knowledge, and sometimes apparent inability to grasp a simple concept, can easily unnerve an impatient trainer. This, in turn, causes emotional upset between the trainer and the trainee which will hinder the learning process. Enthusiasm is contagious and it helps motivate the trainee to learn. Imagination is extremely helpful in the training process because the imaginative trainer will devise new and better ways of explaining and presenting concepts visually. The training program will be in a continual state of improvement.

Willingness to train. The one selected to train may be knowledgeable, able to communicate effectively, and have the desired personal qualifications. If for some reason, he or she does not want to train, however, the training process will not be completely successful. Forcing people against their will to do a job, particularly one which by its nature influences others, is unwise. They must be motivated. Sometimes this unwillingness can be changed if the reason is isolated and eliminated. It is well worth the manager's time to investigate reasons for unwillingness if the would-be trainer possesses all the other qualifications. Often the reasons for unwillingness to train are more imaginary that real. For example, the potential trainer may incorrectly view himself as inadequate in some way. With proper encouragement, praise, and consultation, this imaginary reason can be eliminated.

Summary

A program for effective training must be comprehensive. The trainee must be capable of and motivated toward learning the subject. The bank supervisor must organize a program for training that is consistent with the way people learn—namely, the subject matter must be prepared and presented in an organized and complete manner, effective practice sessions must be devised and scheduled, and the trainee must be constantly evaluated throughout the program. Finally, the program for training requires a trainer who is knowledgeable about the subject, who can communicate effectively, who has the right personal qualifications, and who is willing to train.

Because the training process is complex, the bank manager must take an active role in its development and implementation. Even though this process is difficult and time-consuming, the rewards are great. Well-trained employees are a credit to themselves, the manager, the department, and the bank. The department will operate efficiently and smoothly. The manager will save considerable amounts of time by eliminating those day-to-day problems that always arise in a department that is staffed with poorly trained employees.

Developing Employees

There are no greater personal rewards for a manager than those derived from guiding an employee around the pitfalls of error and upwards onto the paths of success in a banking career. The process of developing people to perform their work to the best of their abilities and to progress from simple jobs to the more advanced functions of banking is complex. The most fundamental principle involved is the manager's genuine interest in developing people. The manager must understand that the bank's greatest assets are the employees. Without the employees there would be no bank. Just because only few employees will rise to positions in higher management is no reason to condemn the majority to work at a level of success below their capabilities. This is a waste of the employees' talents and the bank's resources. Managers have an obligation to the employees in their department, and to the bank, to help the people on their staff to perform and grow as much as they can.

As in all management functions concerning people, the function of employee development must be approached by the manager on a person-to-person basis. All people are not the same. They do not have the same capabilities. They do not have the same personalities. They do not have the same interests. Each person has to be considered individually and developed individually by the manager. An obvious prerequisite of this development function is the manager's genuine and communicated interest in each person, in his or her desires, capabilities, interests and the like.

There are four factors involved in developing an employee.

1. Determining the employee's capabilities;
2. Determining the employee's job interests;
3. Relating the employee's capabilities and job interests with background;
4. Establishing goals to activate the developmental process.

Determining an Employee's Capabilities

Observing an employee on the job day after day is the only effective way of determining capability. It is an ongoing process until a judgement can be made. Even when a judgement is made, it can be made only as of a given time. People are in a constant process of change, and what might be a correct judgement about a person today might not be correct several months in the future. This is particularly true of young people who are still maturing and who are often rapidly changing their work status, or their social status (from single life to married life to parenthood), or their educational status (from high school to college to graduate school).

When a manager is judging the capability of a person in a working situation, certain basic factors should be considered and related to the individual's potential growth within the organization as well as to the job he or she performs.

Quality of work—the thoroughness, accuracy, and neatness of completed jobs.

Quantity of work—the volume of output as compared with objective standards for the experience level of a particular employee.

Dependability—the degree to which an employee applies himself on his own without the need of constant supervision; dependability includes the extent of absenteeism or tardiness.

Judgement—the wisdom of decisions in the absence of detailed instructions. (Generally, this factor is difficult to determine in many of the first-level clerical banking jobs; these jobs usually do not require any appreciable level of judgement.)

Cooperation—the degree to which an employee works harmoniously and effectively with fellow employees, supervisors, and others in the bank.

Attitude—the employee's interest in the job and the bank.

Appearance—the impression made upon others (personal grooming and dress).

Contact Ability—courtesy, tact, pleasantness, and willingness to help other people (employees and customers), including the ability to express oneself effectively with others.

Many banks have a system for rating employees with regard to these factors. Some systems assign point values from zero to five for each factor, and the manager judges which number to use to rate an employee. Other systems employ words like below average, average, above average, and outstanding. These rating systems are an attempt to organize, in writing, the appraisal of an employee's performance. Unfortunately, too much emphasis is placed upon completing these highly structured employee rating forms. What should be emphasized is the importance of identifying those areas in which the employee shows strength and which, therefore, will aid in his development, and those areas in which the employee needs to improve so as not to hinder his development. Determining an employee's performance with regard to these factors should be considered a tool in developing employees, and not merely an exercise in documenting performance for the personnel files.

In judging the performance and capabilities of employees, managers have to be always aware of a phenomenon which occurs quite naturally. It is known as the "halo" effect. The halo effect is the allowing of one positive or negative factor or incident to color (cast a halo on) one's judgement of the overall performance of an employee. An employee who is frequently tardy, for example, should not necessarily be judged as a poor performer overall. An employee who once made an error in judgement should not be condemned by the manager forever. The personal tastes and prejudices of a manager can often create a subtly positive or negative halo. Some personal tastes can take the form of fetishes. These have no direct effect on the work to be performed. A supervisor's strong desire that everyone in the department wear shoes that are always highly polished, for example, is such a fetish. A manager's prejudices against certain classes of people or toward people who are physically attractive, for example, are not only unfair but often illegal.

Determining an Employee's Job Interests

Managers often make the mistake of prejudging an employee's job interests. The only way of knowing for certain how an employee feels about the type of work he or she is doing now and would like to do in the future is to ask the employee. This requires direct communication with the employee, and that is the heart of the development process.

Answers to the following questions will help determine the degree of interest the employee has in being developed.

1. How do you like banking?
2. What areas of banking interest you most?
3. Have you been thinking about a career in banking?
4. What are your short-range job goals?
5. What are your long-range job goals?
6. Have you considered increasing your knowledge of banking through independent reading or enrolling in banking-related night courses?
7. What steps have you taken or would you like to take on-the-job to increase your knowledge of banking?

The answers to these questions certainly will determine in the manager's mind the extent to which the employee is interested in being developed. In fact, each question in itself can be a whole topic of discussion with an employee. Curiously, the process of discussing the topics presented in these questions can and should serve as a simultaneous effort to awaken and increase an employee's interest in development. The employee, for example, may not know enough about banking to be able to answer intelligently the question concerning areas of banking that interest him most. An explanation of the various jobs in the department or of other departments in the bank could follow and perhaps prompt a positive response towards a specific banking interest.

Most jobs in a bank involve either dealing with people or numbers or both. If an employee does not like working with either people or numbers, he probably shouldn't be in banking. Interests centered around people suggest customer service jobs. Interests centered around the use of numbers suggest back office jobs in check clearing, investments, accounting, credit administration, and the like. For those who have at least good facility with numbers and genuine interest in people, more advanced customer service positions, loan work, or possibly jobs involving the management of people are suggested. This is not to say that only an interest in people and numbers is required for many of these jobs; but at least it serves as a useful way to conduct a probing discussion of job interests.

The question concerning interest in the career aspects of banking could lead toward many avenues of discussion. If, for example, the employee plans to work only a couple of years and, for this reason, has a low level of interest in being developed, the employee should be encouraged to make good use of the time while on the job. Many employees, who have started employment with the idea of working for only a short period of time, have stayed with a bank for several years. Banking is a profession that is universal in nature; it can be used in almost any city or town. A female employee may plan to quit work sometime in the future to start a family. She should be reminded that whatever is learned now will not be forgotten. Many women reenter the job market after years of not working for a variety of reasons—their family is grown, their children are in school, their mind and talents are not being used, they need income to help support the family, etc. Whatever is done now to develop a profession is like money in the bank to draw upon in the future.

Relating Capabilities and Job Interests with Background

Once the employee's capabilities and job interests have been identified, the manager can then proceed to relate them to the employee's job experience and education. This part of the development process always should include a discussion about the employee's strong points regarding performance that would aid in his development. It should also include discussion of those performance problems that could seriously hinder development. It should be noted that serious performance problems should be addressed at the time of occurrence and not be delayed until an employee development discussion. They are discussed in a development session mostly as a reminder that they could hinder future progress.

Relating the employee's capabilities with job interests, job experience, and educational background is not as difficult as it may seem, at least with the majority of employees. The following example shows how these factors are easily brought out and related in a discussion with the employee.

Mary Simon has been with the bank for two years in the new accounts department. After graduating from college with an education major, Mary took the job in the bank because there were no teaching jobs available. In a discussion about her job interests it was determined that Mary had a sincere interest in developing herself in banking and would like more responsible work in the area of customer service and/or employee relations. In fact, when the manager explained the nature of management work in the field of bank operations, Mary became quite excited. The manager then proceeded to relate these job interests to Mary's performance, experience, and education. The manager's comments to Mary were as follows:

"Mary, we have been delighted to have you working in the new accounts department during the past two years. Your pleasant, cheerful, helpful ways towards customers and the other employees in the department have been noticed and appreciated not only by myself but by other officers in the bank with whom you have been in contact. Even though your experience so far in banking has been limited to the new accounts department, you have learned much about the services the bank offers and how to be of service to customers. You should not consider your college degree a waste just because it was not business or banking related. The self-discipline you developed in obtaining that education will always be with you to draw upon in the future. The many liberal arts courses you took will add to your general background, and you will be surprised how this knowledge will help you, especially in dealing with people, as you develop in banking.

"I'm sure you realize, Mary, that to develop in any profession a person must be dedicated to learning as much about that profession as possible. This learning takes the form of on-the-job training in combination with outside education. We at the bank can help you with the on-the-job training part of your development as we will discuss later. Only you, however, can increase your knowledge of banking from outside educational sources. As you do not have any formal education in business, we at the bank would strongly recommend that you acquire some if you wish to someday become a part of management. The bank can help you financially with this outside education, but you, of course, have to be interested in devoting some of your free time to this effort.

"Also, Mary, there is one other factor that should be briefly mentioned that could hinder your development. During the past six months you have been absent from the bank quite often. From our other discussions about this you've indicated that this was caused by a serious family problem. Has this problem been resolved?" Mary answered that the problem had indeed been finally and permanently resolved two weeks ago and that she was now free to concentrate all her efforts toward her job. The manager then expressed pleasure and relief that this problem, which would have seriously hindered her development if it continued, was resolved.

The manager then asked Mary how she felt about what had been said so far. Mary responded favorably to all the points mentioned and added that she had been thinking seriously about continuing her education by taking some outside courses. She also asked what the bank could do to give her more on-the-job experience.

Establishing Goals to Activate the Developmental Process

Few employees plan very far into the future concerning their own job development. Employees should be encouraged to develop at least short-range goals, even if the goal is simply to learn a new skill or increase their ability in a known skill. Goals are a kind of map of the future. Without this map, a person could wander aimlessly through months and years on a job. A manager can help an employee establish meaningful job goals to increase skills and knowledge of banking. Ideally, a long-range goal such as Mary Simon's—to become part of the management team in bank operations—should be established first. Then short-range goals are established to reach the long-range goal. Once the long-range goal has been achieved, a new long-range goal can be established and then supported by its set of short-range goals. This process should continue throughout a person's career until his or her maximum potential is achieved.

The most important ingredient in goal setting is the establishing of a time frame within which the goal is to be completed or accomplished. Wide time frames are sufficient for long-range goals. Well-defined time frames are required, however, for short-range goals. The object of goal setting within defined time frames is to commit both the manager and the employee to a course of action. This organized commitment activates the development process. In establishing goals, the manager must consider the employee's job interests, performance, job experience, and educational background.

Let's continue with our hypothetical situation (the Mary Simon case). The manager now proceeds to establish goals in order to activate the development process. These will be short-range goals to support Mary's long-range goal of becoming a part of management. In Mary's case the only hindering performance factor involved, her recent absentee record, apparently has been resolved. No goal setting regarding performance is required at this time. Her awareness that the manager will be watching her future absence record should be sufficient.

Concerning Mary's education goals: After exploring the range of courses that can be taken in local colleges and the American Institute of Banking (AIB), Mary decided to take a series of AIB courses which would be paid for by the bank. The first course she would take would be Principles of Bank Operations to be offered next semester. This would be followed by

Principles of Accounting. No further education goals were to be established until these two courses were completed.

The manager then suggested an immediate goal of learning more about banking through on-the-job experience. Within a month the manager promised that, through a job switch, Mary would be given an opportunity to learn another customer service job within the department, and that the employee doing the other job would be learning and doing Mary's job.

Now that goals were established, the development session with Mary ended. Both Mary and the manager were pleased that a commitment for action had been established. Both parties also agreed that other sessions like this would be conducted in the future as Mary's progress continued and goals were accomplished. To be specific, the next session was to be conducted no later than six months from now.

Ways of Developing Employees on the Job

Job switching and crosstraining. In the case of Mary Simon, the manager chose the job switching method to expose Mary to a different job experience. This is a useful technique if a manager has two different jobs on approximately the same level, and two employees who are willing and able to switch jobs. Switching two employees into each other's jobs does not necessarily have to be done on a permanent basis. It can be done for vacation purposes or as part of a departmental policy of crosstraining to add depth to every employee's background. Crosstraining is teaching each employee as much about each other employee's job as possible. This helps to keep the department running smoothly when there is a temporary shortage of help, and it gives each employee a better knowledge of the functions of the department. It is an obviously effective tool in developing employees.

Job rotation and job enrichment. Allied to the job switching and crosstraining techniques for developing employees on the job are the techniques of job rotation and job enrichment. In job rotation an employee is exposed to a variety of different jobs in a department, usually starting with those at a lower level of responsibility and then graduating to those at higher levels. The rotating of jobs is usually done according to a predetermined schedule. A typical example of job rotation is the management training program wherein the trainee jumps from job to job in several departments, performing each job long enough to understand its content. In job rotation, the employee doing the rotating is often extra to the staff and, therefore, an additional expense to the department's salary budget—a luxury not often found in many bank departments. But if a department has extra staff, even if only on a temporary basis, the job rotation technique can be used very successfully to develop highly capable employees.

Job enrichment refers to adding responsibilities of a higher level to an existing job. Thus the job and the employee performing the job are enriched. This technique is relatively simple to implement. Secretaries, for example, can be given the responsibility of writing their bosses' letters. New account clerks can be trained as savings counselors, given the knowledge of how the bank's certificate-of-deposit interest rates compete with interest rates at savings and loan associations and with the yields on treasury bills, bonds, and notes. More experienced tellers can be given the responsibility of higher check-cashing limits or for balancing the teller department cash at the end of the day. Proof operators can be trained to perform research regarding cash-letter adjustments. Checkfile clerks can be given the added responsibility of answering general telephone inquiries concerning checking accounts.

Job enrichment can be implemented also by assigning a project or parts of a project to an employee. This is a common practice in executive secretarial jobs where often the statistical research or the scheduling of a project is assigned to the secretary. Though not often done by a first-level manager, assigning parts of a managerial project to a clerical employee can be a very effective developmental technique. There is a danger, however, in singling out one employee to do special assignment work. Some of the other employees who were not chosen will want to know why. A plausible reason for selecting one out of many should be developed before this technique is implemented.

This will protect not only the manager from giving the impression of playing favorites, but also the employee from being labeled a favorite.

Promotion. The most obvious way to develop employees is to promote them. Promotion is a definite and permanent change in the job duties of an employee to a higher level of responsibility. Promoting an employee not only gives him an increased level of responsibility and a new learning experience, but it also serves as a powerful motivator. The recognition showered on an employee who has been promoted fires up the employee's interest in the job and in his further development. Although promoting employees is an obvious developmental technique, many managers have difficulty applying it. Managers often do not look in their own backyard for those employees in the department who could be promoted from within. Periodic developmental sessions with each employee will cure this problem. Through these sessions managers become more aware of each employee's capabilities and interests and will be inclined to match employees to promotional openings when they occur. Managers should not be reticent to recommend capable interested employees within their departments as candidates for openings in other departments. To hide a capable employee from the eyes of other managers creates an unhealthy environment in the long run for the manager, the employee, and the bank. Sooner or later the employee involved will react to not being promoted fast enough; he will be lost to the manager either when he terminates employment with the bank or when he is promoted around the manager by one in higher authority. The manager should not delay in recommending an employee who is ready for promotion. The manager will get credit for developing the employee. The employee will move along at a natural pace. Other employees will see this movement and will be encouraged in their own development. The bank will operate more efficiently through its developing employees.

Posting job openings. Many banks have adopted the practice of posting job openings on bulletin boards for all employees in the bank to see and consider. A short description of the job and any education or experience requirements are shown in the posting. Employees are instructed whom to contact if they wish to apply for the job. Managers in bank departments can also adopt the same practice with openings in their own departments. This procedure becomes more practical to adopt in larger departments where there are a variety of jobs being performed. Posting job openings in a department leads to the increased movement of employees from one job to another as openings occur. These movements are usually lateral into jobs of the same level of responsibility but with different duties. At best they could be classified as minor promotions into slightly higher levels of responsibility. Transferring employees from one job to another of similar responsibility, as openings occur, is still another technique in development. Transferring can be done, of course, regardless of whether the openings are posted or not.

In summary, the ways of developing people with regard to on-the-job experience are numerous. They include job switching, crosstraining, job rotation, job enrichment, promotion, posting job openings and transferring. A department manager has to be able to choose the appropriate technique to suit the situation.

Problems in Developing Employees

The subject of posting job openings introduces a major problem which often surfaces when a developmental program for all employees begins—how does a manager handle an employee who is very much interested in development and advancement, but who is limited, at least presently, in capabilities? This problem presents itself in many forms depending on the employee involved. There is no blanket answer. The problem has to be considered in relation to the employee. As has been said before, a manager is a manager of individual people not a group of people who all react exactly the same way to the same situation. The majority of these problems arise with younger employees (not necessarily younger in age but rather those employees who have less than about five years seniority with the bank). Employees with more seniority have settled into their jobs and have usually by this time developed reasonable views of their capabilities in relation to promotional opportunities.

The following case histories should be helpful in coping with typical problem situations that can arise.

1. Sam Reynolds is married and in his late twenties. He was hired three years ago as a universal teller. Eighteen months ago he was promoted to cash teller. Sam is a responsible and well-liked employee. He has had no education beyond high school. Recently, he has been hounding the manager about promotional opportunities. In a session with Sam the manager discovered that Sam was interested in promotional opportunities to earn more money in order to support his taste for the better things in life. The manager then proceeded to advise Sam that employees are promoted in the bank because of accomplishments and efforts that indicate ambition and not because of the amount of salary they wish to earn. The manager further explained that almost everybody wants to earn more money to possess the better things in life. He explained that it is a fact of life that those who are promoted and earn more money are those who are dedicated to the principle of self-development.

The manager continued with rhetorical questions: "Why haven't you developed yourself educationally since you left high school? When was the last time you offered to stay around and help a teller find a difference? When did you show interest in learning more about the other areas of the bank? When did you request a higher check-cashing approval authority, or offer to help me schedule tellers? "

"These are only examples of the many things you could have done to show real interest in development. There is nothing wrong with wanting to earn more money. This want, however, has to be backed up with effort, otherwise it is mere wishful thinking."

This approach to Sam's problem will make Sam think about which path he should follow in the months to come. Whichever way he decides, he will have a better understanding of what to expect and why.

The lack of ambition is a major hindrance to anyone's development. Many employees daydream about promotions, money, prestige, and the like. They must, with the manager's help, realize that the paths of success are difficult to navigate and require continual effort.

2. Sandra Stevens is twenty-five years old, has been employed in the bookkeeping department for three years, and has worked on several of the desk jobs in the department. Sandra is personable, accurate in her work, and very cooperative with her fellow employees and management. Sandra shows signs of insecurity about herself and her place with others. She has no known special natural abilities related to banking that put her into a class above the other employees.

Recently, Sandra heard that Joyce, the assistant manager of the bookkeeping department, was being promoted to manager of another department. She approached the manager about applying for Joyce's job. The manager told Sandra that he would be glad to talk to her about the job and set up an appointment with her the following day. The manager knew that Sandra could not handle the job and that he would have to convince her somehow that this was not the job for her without hurting her feelings.

The next day, when Sandra came to talk about the job opening, the manager prefaced the discussion by stating that he was happy to talk to her about the opening, but that she should realize there were several other candidates being considered both from within the department and in other departments. The manager then proceeded to describe the duties of the job in detail, with special emphasis on the responsibilities involved in managing other employees—listening to their complaints, solving scheduling problems, developing new training programs, etc. Actually, the manager was accentuating those functions of the job that would probably not appeal to Sandra because of her insecurity with other employees. The manager never had to mention to Sandra that he thought she could not handle the job. Sandra was bright enough to figure out that this was not the job for her because she wasn't really interested in getting involved with other people's work problems. In a few days Sandra voluntarily withdrew her application for the job.

The case involving Sandra is an example of how to deal with

employees' wants for jobs which are not suitable for them. Often, emphasizing job duties that require abilities obviously not possessed by the employee or in which the employee is not interested will automatically discourage the employee from pursuing the matter further. This discouragement is healthy because it comes from the logical thinking of the employee once the duties of the job are known and matched by him to his own knowledge about himself. In Sandra's case, the manager made no direct comments about her inabilities in relation to the opening. He merely guided her thinking about the subject to a logical conclusion.

Sometimes, of course, the employee has to be reminded of his lack of interest or ability in certain areas of work which he has freely expressed to the manager on prior occasions. This is not presented in a critical way but only as a reminder to the employee of what has been admitted in the past. Occasionally, an employee is not aware of his lack of ability as indicated by performance in a certain area. The manager then has to bring up the situation, support the judgment with several concrete examples, discuss it with the employee, and then relate it to the employee's current job wants. The subject of counseling employees about their performance is covered in more detail at the end of this chapter.

3. Helen Roberts has been employed as an encoding clerk in the check clearing department for nine months. She is eighteen years old, personable, more mature than her age would indicate, and intelligent; she gets along with others, does more than her share of work, is taking an AIB course nights, and is ambitious. She has become bored in her job.

This situation presents the manager with a different kind of development problem. Helen has many positive traits; plus she has the impatience of youth. The manager discussed with Helen the good job she has done during the short time she has been with the bank. He said that from what he had seen so far she has a potentially good future with the bank. He also stated that her boredom was not uncommon considering her performance and aptitude. The manager, realizing that he must soon resolve this problem or run the risk of discouraging Helen and perhaps even losing her altogether to another employer, solved the problem by promising to transfer her to another, more interesting job in the department or somewhere else in the bank within the next three months. This gave Helen hope and she was satisfied.

The three month time span was selected because the manager realized that to an eighteen-year-old this is a long but not unreasonable period of time to wait. A person's concept of waiting for future time to elapse changes as he grows older. Three months of waiting time for an eighteen-year-old may equate to six months for a twenty-five-year-old or twelve months for a thirty-year-old. One should not consider these figures, however, as guidelines. They are merely used as examples of how maturity in years changes a person's concept of time.

The key to solving Helen's problem was the manager's promise to act with a deadline. The manager reasoned that something positive had to be done and that three months was the most that Helen would wait. This was certainly a sufficient amount of time to arrange for a job transfer. Helen was satisfied because the manager recognized her capabilities and understood her problem, and she was assured that something would be done about it.

These three examples are common occurrences in managing people. Sam Reynolds typifies those whose career desires far outweigh their work ambition. Sandra Stevens is like many employees who view promotion as candy everybody is receiving and they want it too. When they are told what the responsibilities are in those jobs, their taste for the candy often diminishes or disappears. Helen Roberts is one of those employees who have obvious potential and who accordingly have to be moved along at a sufficient pace to provide them with interest and challenge.

Counseling Employees about Performance

As has been mentioned before, part of developing employees is counseling them on those parts of their performance which hinder their development. Not counseling an employee about performance, however, often has consequences which effect more than just the employee involved. Other employees can be influenced by the person who is not performing well, and that in turn reduces the overall performance of the department. Employees do not work in a vacuum. Their actions affect others. The person who is not precise will, through errors, cause work for others. Poor productivity of one is a burden to all. A negative attitude is contagious, particularly among newer employees. Managers often delay correcting serious performance deficiencies because it is a distasteful managerial duty or because they feel inadequate to cope with these situations. Any delay, however, only permits a continually aggravating effect upon others. What follows is a discussion of how to cope with the more serious types of performance problems.

Most serious problems concerning employees continue to exist because the manager is intimidated by the employee. This often happens with employees who have been in a department for several years and who use their seniority as an excuse to indulge in their negative attitudes and uncooperative habits. The manager must realize that the employees do not run the department. The manager runs the department. Once the manager and the employees realize this, future problems are solved more easily or they may never even present themselves.

Often a new department manager inherits employees with serious problems which were never corrected by prior management. Take the example of the employee who has been in a department for ten years. Behind the scenes this employee displays a negative attitude toward the management of the bank and finds fault with every good thing management tries to do for the employees. The manager must cope with this type of individual not only for the employee's own sake, but also for the well-being of the other employees. A difficulty in handling this type of problem is that the employee involved is two-faced. He displays a cooperative or at least neutral attitude in front of the manager and engages in backstabbing actions when the manager is out of sight and earshot. The manager, having no first-hand knowledge of the negativeness, hesitates to accuse the employee without direct proof. There is no question, however, in the manager's mind that the problem exists. It is a well-known fact among the employees in the department and even in other parts of the bank that this employee engages in these tactics. Managers who have to cope with this situation should realize that they are not working in a court of law. Direct personal proof is not required. The hearsay testimony of many other employees in varying jobs throughout the bank is sufficient. In addition, an observant manager can detect a person's negative attitude in general work-oriented conversations with the employee. A negative person cannot completely hide his attitude from the manager.

The way to approach this situation is to go on the offensive. Start the conversation as if it is an obvious fact that the employee performs in this manner. As an example, let's assume that a manager has had enough of a certain employee's negativeness and is prepared to do something about it. Knowing that the final hours of the work week are the best time to discuss such a serious problem, the manager makes an appointment for the end of the week to see the employee. At the appointed time, the manager might begin as follows.

"I've been thinking a lot about you during the past several weeks in relation to your potential in the department and in the bank. I realize and appreciate the knowledge you possess about this department where you have worked for the past ten years. You are intelligent. Your work is performed accurately and efficiently. You appear to work well with customers. There is one important aspect about you in relation to your job, however, that we should discuss seriously—and that is your attitude. It is my distinct impression that you are not happy working for the bank because of your negative attitude towards management, including myself. This is evidenced by your derisive comments to other employees in the coffee room as reported to me by employees not only in this department but also in other departments. I also detect this attitude more subtly in conversations I've had with you. Don't you like working in the bank?"

At this point, the employee will probably, in amazement, rush to defend himself by countering with, "I can't see why you think this way. I've always done my work well. In fact, last week I convinced a customer to open a new account, and he started this account with a $20,000 deposit."

Continuing with the hard-line approach, the manager states: "We certainly appreciate your efforts in attracting this customer to the bank, but frankly we do not appreciate your negative attitude about the management of this bank, particularly when you try to influence others by displaying this attitude publicly. I've noticed you are more discreet when I'm around. It is the impression you give when I'm not present that is disturbing. If you can't say anything good about the bank, then don't say anything. Negative attitudes have a destructive influence not only upon the person conveying these attitudes, but also upon those who hear them—particularly when a more senior person is the negative person. Seniority, in many young people's minds, translates to credibility. For your own sake and for the well-being of the department I want you to think about what has been at least introduced in this discussion. You should understand, however, that your attitude must change and that there is no option on your part. So start thinking positively about restraining yourself from communicating negative comments to others. Start thinking about all the good things you enjoy about your job and the bank. You will be a much happier person."

The direct approach is generally the only one available to a manager when the employee has been permitted to perform in a particular manner for several years. If in the future the employee does not respond favorably, then a second more powerful conversation must be conducted. In this session the manager should state that since the last discussion no noticeable change has been effected in the employee's behavior and that, if this continues, the manager will be forced to find someone else to do the employee's job. The threat of dismissal will usually motivate an employee with this much seniority to correct his behavior at least to a level acceptable to management. Once the employee finally understands that the manager means business, he or she will usually cooperate.

Another difficult performance problem for a supervisor is one with an older employee who resists change. Most employees who have been working for a number of years in the same environment become very comfortable and secure, and they may resist new procedures, a job transfer, or a physical move to a new location. Assuming that the employee involved is physically and mentally capable of coping with the change, as is usually the situation, the resistance is generally only psychological in nature. The manager should always approach the situation with logical arguments about why the change is needed and what advantages there are in the change that positively affect the employee. This approach, though not highly effective in some cases, should be used to show respect for the employee's reasoning ability. Eventually, the employee should realize that the change is coming anyway whether he likes it or not. If a negative attitude develops and persists too long, a conversation with the employee about negative attitudes will be necessary.

Managers are often prejudiced about older people and their resistance to change. One reason is that older people have a tendency to complain about change more. Their complaints however have nothing to do with their native ability to adapt to the change. In fact, it is often surprising to both the employees involved and to management how well they can and will adapt when no alternatives exist. Managers should be on guard not to prejudge an older person's long term reaction to change on the basis of today's complaints. The world, for example, is full of widows who have lost their husbands and have had to completely change their lifestyles. And most of these people have adapted successfuly to this traumatic change in their lives. Any job-related change is, by comparison, insignificant in its effect upon the employee.

Occasionally, a manager may observe that an employee is emotionally disturbed about something which is affecting his performance. If this temporary disturbance, upon investigation, has been determined not to be work-related but rather related to a family or other personal situation, the manager should use extreme caution in counseling the employee. Managers should not get involved in counseling employee's about their personal problems. They can listen with a sympathetic ear but they should not advise the employee to act in any direction. Only encourage the employee to resolve the problem somehow as soon as possible for peace of mind and to alleviate the performance problem.

It is not prudent for a manager to give advice concerning personal problems, even if requested by the employee. Managers are not qualified psychologists, doctors, family counselors, or social workers. If the advice is given and proves to be incorrect in any way, the employee will blame the manager and possibly the bank itself since the manager by his position represents the bank.

There are some situations that arise concerning performance about which the employee, even with counseling, cannot overcome. Occasionally, an employee will be in a job that is not suited for him. The job may require more intelligence than the employee possesses or the employee's personality may not be suited for the job duties. Since a person cannot change his basic intelligence nor significantly alter his personality, any negative comments communicated to an employee about these factors could easily be considered insulting or could have a devastating effect upon the employee's ego. What makes these situations difficult is that something has to be done to correct the problem, but the real reason for the problem should not be mentioned. Occasionally, the nature of the job can be changed to suit the employee, but more often it is best to remove the employee from the job. Transferring him to a more suitable job, with the explanation that the transfer will permit him to learn more about banking or will offer him the opportunity to be more satisfied and/or less frustrated in his work, is often an answer to the problem. Sometimes there is no practical alternative other than to dismiss the employee from the bank. This is particularly difficult because the manager still should not comment negatively about the person's intelligence or personality. The following example illustrates this difficult problem that can be solved only by termination.

Steve Wilson, who is in his mid-twenties, has been a management trainee in the operations division of a medium-sized bank for two years. He has a masters degree in business administration, is well-liked by employees, and is easy to get along with. He is basically a hard-working cooperative employee. During his training, Steve has worked in the bookkeeping department and the customer service department, and he is currently acting as an assistant to the manager of the teller department.

The problem with Steve's performance is two-fold—he has difficulty in applying banking concepts to real situations, and he lacks a sufficiently forceful personality to manage a bank clerical staff. Steve is aware that his overall performance as a management trainee is at least adequate but not extraordinary. On at least two occasions management has counseled him to try to be more definitive and authoritative in giving directions and instructions to employees. The time has now come, after investing two years of time and money in Steve's development, to end the relationship. Management now has the difficult job of dismissing Steve in such a way so as to reduce to a minimum the negative effect upon his ego. The dialogue between the manager and Steve could be as follows.

"Steve, I would like to talk to you today about you and your future in the bank. As you know, you have been a management trainee for two years now and have worked in several of the bank's operating departments. During the past several weeks you've inquired about when you would be considered for an official position in the bank. To be truthful with you, before you spend any more of your time in our training program, you should be aware of our feelings. This has been a difficult decision on our part because you've been well-liked and industrious in your work. We think that you should not plan on being elected an officer at this time or at any time in the near future. Because of this, we see no need of you wasting your time, and we think that it is in your best interest to start looking for another position, either in another bank or in another industry where your career could progress more rapidly."

Steve, being slightly stunned, countered with, "I don't understand; I thought I was doing good work. I like the bank and its management. I thought I had a home here."

The manager continued with, "Steve, as I'm sure you know, we in management are frequently faced with making judgments for the employee's sake as well as for the bank's sake. Sometimes, we make good judgments. Sometimes, we make poor judgments. But we have to make them. This judgment about you is only made in relation to you and our bank. It is not meant to be related to any other bank or any other industry. We can only decide in relation to our own institution. I know this is a disturbing experience for you, but believe me, your career path, as we see it at this point, is not in this bank. The reasons for this decision are not black and white. There is no deep, dark, ominous reason. Please do not be apprehensive about that. Knowing the bank the way we do, and knowing you, we do not see a match that would be to your best advantage."

Steve interjected with, "Is it because I'm not authoritative enough?"

"That might be part of it, Steve," replied the manager, "but in making these decisions about people, as you will see someday perhaps when you are in management, it is difficult to define a decision like this. It is made based on our experience in matching jobs in our bank with people. Please be assured that this has nothing to do with your personality. We think you're a fine young man and certainly wish you well in your future efforts. Take sufficient time to look for another avenue to pursue your interests. We think, however, that you should be able to find something within thirty days. We do not plan to mention this, of course, to any of our employees. When you find another job you can say, if you wish, that you found something more to your liking. If you don't find another job, you can say you are leaving to find something more to your liking. If I can be of any assistance in helping you find another position, I will be more than willing to do what I can. Be assured that we will give you a good work reference."

There are very few, if any, situations in managing people that are more difficult to handle than this situation regarding Steve. Steve was not doing poor work. He was not absent all the time. He did not have a poor attitude. He was not uncooperative. Steve appeared, however, to lack the type of intelligence required to apply concepts to real situations, and his personality was not forceful enough to manage a staff of people, at least in this bank. Nothing could be gained by telling him this. During the discussion, therefore, neither his intelligence nor his personality was mentioned. Steve did not leave the discussion with a crushed ego. He was bewildered and stunned perhaps, but not defeated. Most young people such as Steve have the ability to bounce back into very responsible positions once they find jobs that are better suited to them.

VI
Motivating

How can employees be motivated to perform better in their jobs?

This question pinpoints the reason why managers should be interested in the subject of motivation. Managers are charged with the responsibility of getting things done through other people. By properly inspiring, influencing, persuading, and moving employees, managers will get more done more accurately in less time. This will add to their own effectiveness in their jobs. Their employees will be working up to their abilities and potential. The customers of the bank will be better served. The bank as a whole will prosper.

During the past quarter century motivation, as it relates to business, has become a popular subject with psychologists, university professors, management consultants, and businessmen. Scores of books and articles on the subject have been written by authors such as Abraham Maslow, Douglas McGregor, Frederick Herzberg, Victor Broom, Julian Rotter, Joseph Scanlon, Peter Drucker, Leon Festinger, David McClelland, and Eric Berne to name but a few. But no one to date has found a magic formula for motivating people. The difficulty with the subject is that motivation involves the study of human nature; and, of all the studies we pursue, the study of ourselves is the most perplexing.

The reason for this is that each man is a complex being composed of different aspects (physical, intellectual, and emotional) which have been influenced by his heredity, rearing, culture, social contacts, knowledge, experiences, and independent thinking. The fact that each person changes to some degree as he passes through the decades from youth to old age does not make this perplexing subject any easier.

But although a veil of mystery still exists about human behavior and motivations, managers should not be discouraged. There are certain behavioral concepts that do shine through this veil. This chapter will explore these concepts, some of which may be obvious but are often overlooked. Rather than theoretic, these basic concepts are practical in nature and represent a common-sense approach to the effective motivation of employees.

Human Nature

In studying the motivation of people it is only prudent that one review briefly what is now known about human nature as it relates to behavior and consequent job motivation. From this review, motivational concepts will be more easily identified. Accordingly, this section will present a series of basic characteristics of human beings and the motivating and demotivating factors associated with them.

As will become apparent, the study of motivation includes the equally important aspect of demotivation. Demotivation is the robbing of a person's natural desire or ability for work. Motivating factors encourage a person toward work; demotivating factors discourage a person from work. Certain techniques are motivating when used by a manager, but equally demotivating when not used at all.

The Physical

The human body requires proper air, wholesome food, sufficient exercise and rest, and adequate shelter in order to be healthy and able to perform well. Both physical and mental performance depend on how well these requirements are met.

Physical Surroundings. Curiously, providing the proper physical surroundings for people in a working environment does little to motivate them to do a job better; but by not providing this environment strong demotivating forces can be created. For example, employees who have to sit in uncomfortable chairs hour after hour, or who work in a continual cold air draft, or who do detail work without sufficient light will, most often, if these conditions are allowed to continue, be demotivated. The quality of their work will diminish. This demotivation is caused not only by these physical discomforts, but also by the knowledge that management ignores these poor working conditions. Thus a negative effect on employee morale is created, as manifested by the comment, "If the manager doesn't care about me, I don't care about the work." Managers, therefore, should be conscious of identifying and correcting those physical aspects of the working environment that cause employee discomfort.

Health. Employees who enjoy good physical health are, at best, mildly motivated to perform well. Employees who are in pain due to illness or accident, however, are strongly demotivated. Their minds automatically focus on the feeling of pain. A headache, for example, which is a common occurrence, can be demotivating, and migraine headaches can be crippling. Employees in pain, regardless of its source, should be encouraged to seek medical relief and not to grin and bear it. It is the only practical solution for the employee's sake and for the sake of the work to be performed.

The Intellectual and Emotional

People have minds which are capable of learning and remembering information. Their minds are then capable of using this knowledge to think (compare, analyze, rearrange, discriminate, investigate, imagine, judge, decide). Because people have intellectual ability, they have a natural inclination to use it. They are curious, they want knowledge, and they are thinking about something during practically every waking moment. Each person's mind is so uniquely designed that it can, in conjunction with the body, receive information through the senses. It can think about this information and communicate the same knowledge or an altered version to other people through the spoken or written word.

Very closely associated with the intellectual side of man is the emotional. Because the mind perceives the outside world to such a high degree, a person can "feel" the sensations of pleasure in a sunset, joy in the birth of a child, sorrow in the death of a friend, fear of a perceived threat, anger at a personal injustice, and love of a parent. These and other emotions are strong motivators for action. People will travel thousands of miles for the pleasure of seeing and experiencing a foreign country, or they will work hours and days on a project with little rest for the joy of creating something new. History is full of examples of what one person will do out of love for another. People require peace of mind, relief from the negative emotions of fear, worry, and apprehension which are caused by life's conflicts and frustrations. If a person experiences negative emotions for too long a period, emotional stability, as well as a normal, peaceful existence, is threatened.

Desire for knowledge. Since man is endowed with a highly developed mind, he is intellectually curious. On the job, he should be given the opportunity and freedom to learn more and more about the job. Each bit of knowledge gives him the desire to acquire more knowledge. Accordingly, training programs and written literature about his job, his department and other parts of the bank should be made available to him. There are some employees who have magnificent minds but who have never been encouraged to use them to their advantage. This encouragement can take the form, for example, of permitting them to think about a common departmental problem and to investigate and suggest solutions.

Peace and quiet. The mind, in order to operate, requires a certain degree of peace and quiet. Noise and interruption are demotivators in relation to mental activity. A person cannot think if his mind is constantly being barraged by outside influences (phones ringing, unnecessary building noises, inconsequential interruptions by other employees, etc.).

Joy. Enjoyment of one's job is a strong motivator. There is no reason why most employees cannot enjoy coming to work and basically want to do their job. If the manager operates a department that is properly organized and if he communicates, trains and motivates well, then the employees will be predisposed to enjoy their work and to work efficiently. This is assuming, however, that each employee is placed in a job which is suitable to his interests, abilities, and talents.

Anxiety. Fear, worry, and apprehension can be both strong motivators and strong demotivators. Anxiety can be caused by factors both related to the job and unrelated to the job. Unfortunately, most employees have difficulty in shutting off their worries and fears from the home when at work, and from work when at home. Managers should realize that home worries can affect job performance negatively; employees should be counseled to eliminate them as soon as possible.

Managers should be constantly alert to those job situations that cause anxiety. Employees can worry or be apprehensive about their lack of ability to perform, their personal relations with fellow workers, and their relations with the manager, to name a few categories. Managers can and should eliminate these job-created anxieties because they decrease performance. A teller who is too worried about having a cash difference is more prone to have differences. The manager should counsel a conscientious teller to stop worrying with the comment such as: "If I'm not worrying about you having a difference, why should you?"

Occasionally two employees cannot get along with one another. This causes anxiety as well as other emotional disturbances for both employees, thus doubling the negative performance effect. Their attentions are focused on their dislike for one another rather than on the work. The manager should step in and, by talking to each employee alone, try to isolate and resolve the problem. If counseling the employees produces no results, the employees should be physically separated to reduce the irritating effect of being in constant social contact with one another. Managers themselves can inadvertently create anxiety problems in employees by forgetting a salary review date, being too busy to see them when they have a work problem, not fulfilling a promise, showing partiality, etc.

In order to eliminate demotivating anxiety situations, managers must constantly be alert to their existence through continual verbal communication with employees. Managers who are too busy or who are away from their departments for long periods of time will not be aware of problems. If the type of situations described above are permitted to exist for a period of time, the employees could easily respond to the frustration with anger, apathy, indifference, or withdrawal. Regardless of the response, the resultant effect is demotivation and consequent poor work performance.

Managers also have the option of inducing anxiety as a motivator of employees. Using fear, for example, in the work environment has been done for centuries. In times past, slaves performed out of fear of being beaten. Even in the early part of this century, managers motivated employees almost exclusively through fear of job loss, salary reduction, loss of privileges, and the like. The use of fear still is a strong motivator but, like the doctor's medicine, it should be used sparingly and in proper doses to suit the individual. Unfortunately, some managers still think that fear and its close cousins, worry and apprehension, are the only managerial motivators of value, and they automatically employ them when a performance problem exists.

As has been and will be shown in this chapter, there are many reasons why employees are not properly motivated to perform. A good manager should consider the solution of the performance problem through all the other motivators before using fear. If, after careful consideration, all attempts to use other motivators or to eliminate demotivators are not fruitful, fear can be used. Because fear can be both a motivator and a demotivator, and because the manager is not a psychologist, the dosage cannot be accurately prescribed in advance for each individual. The best way, therefore, is to start with a weak dosage and, if it is not effective, to increase the strength until the desired effect is obtained.

Employees respond to fear in a variety of ways. To some, a brief statement from the manager that a performance problem has been noticed is sufficient. To others, the direct threat of dismissal from the bank is the only way to motivate. Then there are always a few who won't respond to fear at all. Depending on the problem, of course, there are less drastic fear-related inducements that the manager can use. The most obvious of these are related to salary—reduced raise, deferred raise, or no raise. When these inducements are used, the employee should be told that their use is for purposes of maintaining discipline in the department so that the work will be done properly. They should not be announced in a punishing or vindictive manner.

A supervisor may be tempted to punish employees for wrong doing in an attempt to motivate them towards better future behavior. Susan Rogers, for example, returned fifteen minutes late from lunch one day. The manager, wishing to teach Susan a lesson and to save face with the other employees in the department, told her she would have to work late that night after the others went home. This action was rightfully perceived by the employee as childish punishment and was resented. In the days to come Susan reduced her output to "punish" the manager. The manager succeeded in demotivating Susan, not motivating her. In this instance, counseling Susan about returning from lunch on time would have been sufficient. Punishments, particularly those made without warning, are rarely successful. In fact they usually are demotivating.

Mild forms of anxiety can be used to motivate employees to do a job more thoroughly. This is especially true of project-oriented work. For example, a manager of a new accounts department plans to have an employee meeting and wishes to cover the subject of "Savings Account Interest—Its Computation and Payment." Not having the time to prepare for the meeting, the manager assigns the research for the subject to an assistant. In order to help insure that the subject matter is well prepared he adds, "And by the way, be prepared to present this topic yourself at the meeting." The manager, by requiring the assistant to actually speak about the subject to the employees, induces apprehension. The assistant is thus motivated to prepare the subject better for fear of appearing ignorant in front of others.

The Social

Since time immemorial people have lived in groups, the most basic group being the family. From the family ever-widening groups have been established—neighborhoods, town, counties, states, and nations. People basically like other people; they like living with them and working with them. Part of this affinity for others is due to each person's ability and interest in communicating his thoughts to other people. Conversely, each person learns from the communicated thoughts of others.

Sociologists tell us that man's instincts for regulating his behavior are not as highly developed as in lower forms of animals, and therefore he relies more heavily on social organizations of all types for guidance. Whether for disseminating or acquiring knowledge, or for guidance in behavior, or for other reasons known and unknown, it is obvious that people want to live and work with other people. As a result of this interaction, each person in a group is influenced by the thoughts and actions of the others.

Negative influences. The influence of employees upon one another in a group is a complex subject, and no precise set of rules regarding behavior can be clearly discerned. Some influential factors are evident. The negative attitude of one employee can demotivate other employees—particularly those who are new to the group, or those who are easily lead by a strong personality. Unfortunately, it seems that negative influences are more demotivating than positive influences are motivating. This is merely a statement of opinion and not one based on scientific research. In any event managers should encourage positive attitudes to insure a healthy environment for employees. Negative attitudes should be eliminated with haste either by quieting the employee involved or, if the attitude is caused by a real problem, correcting the problem. Negative attitudes are demotivating because they attack the morale of the whole group. Poor group morale produces poor performance. Parenthetically, the morale of a group of employees is either good or bad in direct relation to the quality of management. It could even be said that good management produces good morale and poor management produces poor morale.

Isolation. Because man is basically social and needs the presence of other people in a working environment, a manager has to be careful not to isolate a clerical employee from contact with other people. Isolation can be a matter of degree, ranging from complete separation from people (no contact, not even by phone) to limited phone and/or personal contact such as might be found in a remote customer banking facility where only two employees are required to staff the area. Keeping an employee out of sight and sound from other people can be demoralizing. In some banking situations a degree of isolation is required, and a manager must be careful to match the social needs of those employees who will be working in these situations to the degree of isolation required.

As a general rule, a group of clerical employees performing routine tasks, such as typists, proof operators, encoding clerks, checkfile clerks, etc., will perform better if they are all located in the same physical environment and not isolated from one another. This grouping of employees provides a certain element of competition among the individuals in the group. Faster employees, for example, enjoy the prestige of being recognized for their ability as observed by the other members of the group. Slower employees are often motivated to try harder to catch up with the others in the group.

Group discipline. Ironically, the presence of managerial discipline and fairness in a department are not strong motivators because they are expected by employees. Their absence, however, is a strong demotivator. In any group work environment, rules of conduct must be instituted to insure that all employees know and do what management requires in relation to the work to be performed. Lack of discipline produces disorder and apathy, and it could lead to unfairness. Unfair managerial practices, surprisingly, will demotivate not only the employee directly involved, but also other employees who have knowledge of the unfairness. This expanded effect is probably due to the logic: "If the manager has been unfair to that person, he will someday be unfair to me." Unfairness produces apathy and disinterest in doing the work because the employee feels cheated of his rights, and he loses a certain amount of respect for the integrity of the manager.

Social events. Finally, all organizations sponsor at least some social, non-work activities such as employee parties and sports events in order to provide employees with the opportunity to meet and socialize with one another. This enables employees to get to know each other; it adds to the solidarity of the group when they meet in the working environment. Employee parties and the like are not strong motivators in themselves but they do provide a great deal of general goodwill which could dispose employees to be more cooperative with one another and with management.

The Individual

Although each person possesses all the characteristics discussed so far, each one is also uniquely different. So the manager must realize that each individual will respond to motivators and demotivators differently, though probably within a broadly defined range. Most people can be motivated by fear, for example, but to what degree will depend on the individual.

Another useful fact to remember is that people naturally recognize their own individuality more fully than that of others, and they take a very natural interest in themselves. For this reason, each person likes to be called by name and to talk about his own ideas, family, car, house, vacation, experiences, and achievements.

Recognition and praise. The concept of each person's individuality introduces to the manager an array of powerful motivators. The most obvious motivators related to individuality are praise and recognition. Through sincere and honest praise and recognition a manager can motivate employees literally to move mountains. Unfortunately, these motivators are often not used to their full potential by the bank department manager. Employees are more often reprimanded for what they do wrong, rather than praised for what they do right.

Praise and recognition can take many forms, ranging from verbal compliments to increased salary, promotions, titles, job enrichment, etc. Often a simple unexpected verbal compliment such as, "I'm glad you're working in this department. You have an outstanding way of dealing with customers," or "You're doing a super job in this department. Keep up the good work" will go a long way toward motivating an employee to continue his or her good work in the weeks to come. Money, titles, and promotions show recognition of a job well done and are also effective for motivating future performance if the employee is a good performer and the recognition is well deserved. But dangling these prizes in front of a poor performer in the hopes of improving performance has mixed motivational results and is highly dependent on the individual involved. To use money as an example, the poor performer who is confronted with the alternative of performing better on the job or forfeiting a salary increase may improve his performance long enough to obtain the salary increase, and then regress to former poor performance habits. Generally speaking, money, titles, promotions, and the like are better motivators of future performance if they are used to recognize an already good worker rather than to bribe a poor worker. Conversely, withholding these tangible forms of recognition from the well-deserved can be very devastating to their morale and cause demotivation.

To illustrate the motivating power of praise and recognition, a true story should be told of what happened years ago in the proof and transit department of a medium-sized, multibranch eastern bank. The manager of the department at that time was intrigued with the subject of how to motivate the proof operators to process more items per day through the machines.

In those days the multipocket proof machines were constructed in such a way that, as the checks were added, the operator would press one of twenty buttons to activate a flap which covered the particular pocket into which the checks were to be placed. There were twenty of these pockets surrounding the keyboard and as the operator's right hand would index the amount of each check and activate the flap over the pocket, the left hand was used to physically place the check in the pocket. Since there were twenty pockets, the location of many of them were almost beyond the reach of the operator's left arm and hand. The reaching involved in placing these checks into the correct pocket was at times physically strenuous.

There was a counter on each machine that automatically registered the number of items that the operator processed as they were being processed. The counter which was reset to zero each morning could register up to 9,999 and then would roll over to 0,000 indicating that the operator had processed 10,000 items that day. Added to the speed factor of processing 10,000 items was an accuracy factor. The checks were added in batches, and each batch had to be balanced to the penny. If the operator was inaccurate in indexing the amount of the checks, thus causing an out of balance condition, the operator would have to stop the machine, look for the difference, and correct it before continuing. A fast but inaccurate operator, therefore would waste too much time looking for differences and could never reach the 10,000 item mark. Consequently, because of the physical layout of the machine and the combined speed and accuracy factors, processing 10,000 items in a single day was a difficult accomplishment. It wasn't very often that any of the eleven proof operators in this department accomplished this feat. There was one veteran operator, however, who on occasion would roll over the machine thus signifying the processing of 10,000 items. When this happened the manager and the other employees in the department would notice and marvel at the skill of this employee.

The manager of the department, having assigned himself the project of devising a way to motivate all the proof operators to process more items through the machines, focused his thoughts on the magic of the 10,000 item mark—an ambitious motivational goal! The manager thought of the more traditional ways of recognizing efforts with money, gift awards, lists of names on the bulletin board, etc., but he discarded them as being too cumbersome and possibly ineffective. Finally, the manager decided to keep the whole thing simple, and remembering his grade school days, went out to the ten-cent store on his lunch hour one day and bought one package each of green and black construction paper and a box of large gold stars. After work that day, when all the employees had gone home, he cut out from the green paper three by nine inch placards, and from the black paper, two by eight inch placards. The black placards were pasted on to the green ones thus creating a green border around the black. In the middle of the black field one large gold star was pasted. Several of these signs were made, placed in an envelope, and put in the manager's desk for safe-keeping.

The object of making these signs was that the next time an operator reached 10,000 items, the manager would take one of them from his drawer and attach it to the operator's machine for all to see—a sort of "badge of skill." No one knew what the manager had in mind. There was no announcement, no fanfare. Several days went by. Then one Friday the work was heavy, and the veteran operator was running fast. By noon she had approached 6,000 items, by 2:30 she reached 8,000 items, and finally at 4:30 she rolled over her machine—10,000 items. It was time for the gold star. The manager was fearful. Was this too simple, too childish an idea? Would it backfire? Was this the right type of praise and recognition? Mustering his courage, he took a sign out of his desk, walked over to the operator, and attached it on her machine. The operator looked up quizzically and wanted to know what it was. The manager merely said, "It's a gold star for rolling over your machine. Congratulations!" The operator smiled a little, and then the manager walked away. At the end of the day some of the other operators happened to walk by her machine and, noticing the gold star, asked the operator what it was. The seeds of motivation had been sown.

The very next business day the same operator rolled over her machine again. The manager went over to her machine with his box of gold stars and pasted another one next to the first. The sign had been designed to hold a maximum of five gold stars in a line on the field of black. Within two weeks there were five gold stars on that operator's sign. Also during this time, something magical was happening. Production was up among the other operators. Within a month three other operators received their first gold stars. At the end of three months all the operators had their "badge of skill." Many of the operators struggled hard to get their gold stars. On many days there wasn't enough work for any operator to process that many items. At the end of six months the veteran operator had been awarded over fifty gold stars; the whole side of her machine was decorated with signs each filled with gold stars. During this period everyone in the bank became aware of the gold star awards and would come into the department to see them and praise the operators. The manager was pleased. The motivator of praise and recognition had worked. In fact it had " moved mountains."

Criticism. If praise and recognition motivate, condemnation, ridicule, or debasement will demotivate. Typical of this in a working environment is a manager's criticism of an employee in front of others. Critical remarks attack a person's ego and self-image, and they are demotivating. Critical remarks made in front of others multiply the demotivating effects because they attack the employee's self-image as it relates to others. Constructive, helpful criticism is, of course, required at times, but it should always be done in private.

Setting goals. The story about the gold stars introduces another motivator that is related to individuality—goal setting. As was discussed in the last chapter, employees will be motivated to perform a function better if they know what is expected of them. Performance standards should be determined for each job and explained to the employee. The manager then should watch to see that these standards are met by the employees. Without goals, employees will vary widely in their performance from day to day, or will set their own goals which often do not in any way correspond to those that management would perceive as challenging or even adequate. The concept of the individuality of each person suggests that goal setting be individualized. It is fine to have overall departmental goals, but it is each individual, as a part of the whole, who is going to fulfill these goals. The manager must relate an overall goal to individual shares. This fixes responsibility upon the individual. In reality, overall goals are accomplished by individual efforts.

Freedom. Finally, each employee, because of his individuality, should be given the freedom to express his individuality. This encompasses many specific freedoms. Predominant among these are freedom to express one's ideas and suggestions, freedom to defend oneself, freedom to achieve, freedom to advance in the organization, and freedom to learn. These freedoms will motivate the employees to use their own talents as they develop.

Summary

The subject of motivation is many faceted. Because people are individuals, the motivators and demotivators described in this chapter will influence employees in varying degrees, depending upon the motivator, the situation and the employee. The manager has the difficult task of choosing the correct motivator (or isolating and eliminating the demotivator) in relation to the circumstances.

It is apparent that general good management in the organizing, communicating, and training functions of management will motivate, and poor management in these areas will demotivate. To be more specific, good managers will recognize the motivational values of freedom to learn, properly induced anxiety, praise and recognition, job enjoyment, goal setting, and freedom of expression. In addition, good managers will be aware of those specific factors that will demotivate such as physical discomfort, unhappiness in the job, anxiety, negative influences of others, isolation, ridicule, lack of discipline, and unfairness. Finally, the underlying principle of influencing others towards proper action is the manager's general, communicated interest in the well-being of each employee. The individuality of man demands that each person be recognized as an individual and managed accordingly.

VII
Using Statistics in Management

First-level bank managers are often unaware of the important role statistical information can play in both the short-range and long-range management of their departments. Statistics, properly compiled and maintained, are roadmaps showing where a department has been and where it is going. Statistics can give a department supervisor measurements of work loads and thus staffing requirements. Statistics can give comparisons of costs and revenues and thus show how a department is doing in relation to the past, to other departments in the bank, or to other banks. Some supervisors have a tendency to make important decisions regarding staffing, scheduling, cost control, and departmental procedures without the benefit of proper research. This research should always include the accumulation and interpretation of departmental statistical information.

Types of Statistical Records

In general, there are four major categories of statistical records that should be compiled by a department supervisor—volume statistics, income statistics, expense statistics, and personnel statistics. Figure 7 shows a sample listing of the kinds of statistical items that a manager of a teller department would find useful in the four statistical categories. Each department in a bank should accumulate pertinent statistical information. In the new accounts department, for example, the number of ac-

Figure 7
Statistical Items—Teller Department

VOLUME STATISTICS

Number of:
Lobby transactions
Walkup transactions
Drive-in transactions
Total teller transactions
Drive-in cars
Mail teller transactions
Night depository transactions
Utility payments accepted
Cashiers checks issued
Money orders sold
Savings bonds issued
Travelers check packages sold
Teller differences
Business checking accounts serviced
Personal checking accounts serviced
Regular savings accounts serviced
Premium type savings accounts serviced
Total accounts serviced

INCOME STATISTICS

Income from:
Cashiers checks issued
Travelers checks sold
Money orders sold
Utility payments accepted

EXPENSE STATISTICS

Dollar amount of:
Net teller differences
Employee salaries
Overtime paid
Fees waived
Fraudulent check losses
Other losses
Total losses

PERSONNEL STATISTICS

Number of full-time employees
Number of part-time employees
Number of employee absence days
Number of overtime hours worked
Turnover rates (full-time employees)

counts by type that were opened and closed should be compiled. In the installment lending area, the number of applications for loans processed (accepted and rejected), the number and dollar amount of loans by type on the books, and statistics concerning delinquent and charged-off loans are important. In the bookkeeping department, statistics concerning the number of open checking accounts by type, the number of deposits and checks posted, and the amount of service charges collected by type should be accumulated. In the check clearing department, items processed per operator, the number of machine operator errors, and machine down-time due to mechanical failure should be tabulated. Typical of the statistics that should be kept in the safe deposit department are the number of boxes rented and vacant, the number of entries into boxes, the number of customers who opened new box-accounts and who closed accounts, and the dollar amount of income earned by box size.

Personnel statistics are similar in all departments of a bank. All managers should know the number of employees in their department and the employee turnover rates. In addition, managers should maintain subsidiary records for each employee showing salary history, absence from work, and volume and accuracy of work performed.

Sources of Statistical Data

When first confronted with the job of gathering departmental statistical data, a supervisor might not realize the amount of record keeping that already goes on in the bank. The single most important source of statistical data for all departments is computer records. Daily, weekly, and monthly computer printouts almost always contain summary pages for each report which shows volumes for every category of item processed. A manager can almost be certain that if the department's work is processed by a computer, important volume statistical information will be shown on some computer report.

Departments that interconnect with all other departments such as the control department, the personnel department, and the auditing department often keep records that can be of help to a department manager. Bank business machines such as those used to microfilm checks, process proof and transit items, and process teller items all have automatic counters from which volume statistics can be obtained. Only after these potential sources of data are fully explored should the manager resort to the obvious, but laborious, method of compiling the data by hand on a daily basis. Even if the hand-count method is the only way of obtaining specific information, each employee performing the work can be asked to count his own items processed during the day and report the information to the manager on a periodic basis.

Statistical Report Formats

The most common and practical time frame for the accumulation and reporting of departmental statistical data is the month. From monthly reports quarterly and yearly reports can be easily compiled. Figure 8 shows a monthly statistical report that could be compiled in a teller department using the listing of statistical items shown in figure 7. There are six columns of information for each item listed—the current month's statistics as compared to the same month a year ago (columns 1 and 2), an accumulation of all months during the current year as compared to last year (columns 3 and 4; since this is a December report, a twelve month accumulation is shown), and the variance between the two year-to-date accumulation columns shown in numbers (column 5) and in percentages (column 6). At the bottom of the report, as part of the personnel statistics, the employee turnover rates are shown for 1978 and 1977 by quarter rather than monthly. When showing statistics for small numbers, quarterly reports are more practical and meaningful than monthly reports.

The figures shown in figure 8 are presented as an example of how statistical information would look in this report format. The relationships between the figures are reasonable and could exist in a bank's teller department, but they are not to be considered a norm as they are presented for display purposes only.

Although the completed report shown in figure 8 appears massive in content and difficult to compile, in actuality columns 2 through 6 of this report should only take about two hours to complete each month. Columns 2 and 4 are merely copied from last year's December report. Column 3 is compiled by adding last month's column 3 figure to this month's column 1 figure. Column 5 is the difference between columns 3 and 4; and column 6 is calculated by dividing the figure in column 5 by the figure in column 4. The most time-consuming part of preparing this report is column 1, the current month's statistics. Considerable time can be saved in gathering the data necessary to complete column 1, however, if certain volume statistics are compiled on a daily basis. For example, transaction counts can be accumulated daily from teller machine tapes. The volume of various items sold or issued (money orders, traveler's checks, savings bonds, cashiers checks) can be obtained from daily inventory control records. Volume statistics regarding the number of accounts serviced, and income, expense, and personnel statistics can be obtained for the most part from existing monthly computer, general ledger, and personnel records.

Statistical reports are more meaningful when the data is accumulated over several months and compared to previous years' reports. It is the comparison that provides the trends. The more historical data that is available, the better the comparison and the more defined the trends become. Interpreting statistical reports is a managerial function that can provide more in-depth knowledge about a department. An important column of information in the report shown in figure 8 is column 6—the percentage variance over the previous year's performance. It is interesting to compare the previous year's activity with this column and to note the following.

1. The volume of transactions in the drive-in and walk-up has increased almost twice as much as in the lobby.
2. The number of traveler's check sales (an important income producing service for the department) has not increased in relation to other teller activity.
3. The number and amounts of teller differences have only increased in direct relation to the increase in activity.

Figure 8
Monthly Statistical Report—Teller Department December 1978

Volume Statistics #	(1) December 1978	(2) December 1977	(3) Year To Date 1978	(4) Year To Date 1977	(5) Year To Date Yearly Var.	(6) Year To Date Yearly % Var.
Lobby transactions	55,872	48,876	606,100	560,900	+ 45,200	+ 8%
Walkup transactions	11,704	10,353	149,733	130,311	+ 19,422	+15%
Drive-in transactions	27,762	27,100	312,020	270,332	+ 41,688	+15%
Total teller transactions	95,538	86,329	1,067,853	961,543	+106,310	+11%
Drive-in cars	17,218	15,136	206,900	179,444	+ 27,456	+15%
Mail teller transactions	8,011	7,412	95,973	89,538	+ 6,435	+ 7%
Night depository transactions	1,702	1,623	21,103	19,972	+ 1,131	+ 6%
Utility payments accepted	1,572	1,450	19,778	19,501	+ 277	+ 1%
Cashiers checks issued	1,392	1,205	16,553	15,489	+ 1,064	+ 7%
Money orders sold	923	875	11,576	10,978	+ 598	+ 5%
Savings bonds issued	490	450	6,123	6,050	+ 73	+ 1%
Travelers ck. packages sold	1,372	1,350	16,700	16,501	+ 199	+ 1%
Teller differences	183	173	2,210	1,998	+ 212	+10%
Bus. ck. accts. serviced	3,033	2,905	NA	NA	+ 128	+ 4%
Per. ck. accts. serviced	11,720	10,923	NA	NA	+ 797	+ 7%
Reg. sav. accts. serviced	15,003	13,115	NA	NA	+ 1,888	+14%
Prem. type sav. accts. serviced	4,300	3,725	NA	NA	+ 575	+15%
Total accounts serviced	34,056	30,668	NA	NA	+ 3,388	+11%
Income Statistics $						
Cashiers checks issued	317	271	3,713	3,484	+ 229	+ 7%
Travelers checks sold	1,611	1,585	22,031	21,781	+ 250	+ 1%
Money orders sold	210	185	2,865	2,717	+ 148	+ 5%
Utility payments accepted	78	72	988	975	+ 13	+ 1%

Expense Statistics $

Net teller differences	73	412	3,972	3,607	+	365	+10%
Employee salaries	22,200	18,403	270,337	215,836	+	5,450	+25%
Overtime paid	140	0	2,159	1,803	+	356	+19%
Fees waived	153	147	1,712	1,603	+	109	+7%
Fraudulent check losses	372	112	3,725	3,473	+	252	+7%
Other losses	52	0	357	330	+	27	+8%
Total losses	424	112	4,082	3,703	+	379	+10%

Personnel Statistics

# of full-time employees	33	30	33*	27*	+	6	+22%
# of part-time employees	7	5	6*	6*	+	0	+ 0%
# of employee absence days	9	8	76	80	–	4	– 5%
# of overtime hours worked	27	0	363	312	+	51	+16%

Employee Turnover Rates (Full-Time Employees)

	1978	1977
First quarter	6%	6%
Second quarter	10%	9%
Third quarter	13%	9%
Fourth quarter	7%	6%
Total year	36%	30%

Notes:
* = Average number of employees for the twelve month period
NA = Not applicable
Percentages shown have been rounded off to the nearest whole number.

Performance in this area, therefore, has remained constant.
4. Employee turnover has increased substantially.
5. Employee salaries have increased substantially.

These observations should raise the following questions in the manager's mind.

1. Is the drive-in and walk-up properly staffed to handle the increased activity? Are there a sufficient number of drive-in lanes open at all times to handle the increase in traffic?
2. What programs can be developed to increase traveler's check sales?
3. What caused the increase in employee turnover?
4. Has the increase in the average number of employees in the department been caused by the turnover, by the increase in volume, or both? How is this related to the increase in salaries?

Statistical reports become even more meaningful when they show more history. A history of data covering a five-year period is ideal for comparison and trend identification purposes. Figure 9 is a five-year turnover-rate report for the same teller department shown in figure 8.

From this five-year report two things are obviously consistent. The turnover rate has increased each year over the previous

Figure 9
Employee Turnover Rates—Teller Department
(full time employees)

	1978	1977	1976	1975	1974
First Quarter	6%	6%	4%	1%	3%
Second Quarter	10%	9%	10%	7%	9%
Third Quarter	13%	9%	9%	11%	6%
Fourth Quarter	7%	6%	4%	5%	3%
Total Year	36%	30%	27%	24%	21%

year, and turnover in this department is historically higher in the second and third quarters of the year than in the first and fourth quarters. This, of course, would lead the manager to question why and what can be done about it.

The turnover rate of a department is computed by dividing the number of employees who left (twelve for example) by the average number of employees in the department (thirty-three for example) to yield a rate of 36 percent. Turnover rates should be calculated with the average number of employees in the department for the period of time and not the number of employees as of one point in time.

Another common statistic used by bankers is "average number of items processed per employee." This can be shown on a per hour, per day, per week, or per month basis depending on the circumstance. If a group of employees such as tellers, proof operators, encoding clerks, and file clerks are all performing the same function, and they work approximately the same hours, a manager can compute the average number of items processed per employee. If, for example, on a given day, five employees in a proof department processed a total of 33,000 items, and each employee worked 7.5 hours, the average number of items processed per employee per day would be 6600. The average number of items processed per hour per employee would be 880. If each employee was doing his share of the work, the count on each proof machine would be 6600 items at the end of the day. By knowing what each proof machine operator should have processed and comparing it to the actual count of what each operator did process, the manager can determine which employees are doing their share of the work, more than their share, or less than their share. This data is important when the manager is trying to identify the performance of each employee. It serves as method of plotting and developing future goals for departmental performance.

Graphic Statistical Formats

Figures 8 and 9 are examples of the traditional way of presenting statistics. There are occasions, however, when presenting statistics more graphically are desirable. Typical of these occasions are times when a manager wishes to display trends or performance in a specific area to a group of employees or senior management. Rather than show these figures in numbers only, it is very effective visually to show the numbers in graphic form. There are three graphic forms commonly used for illustrative purposes—the bar chart, the pie chart, and the line chart. Bar and line charts are useful in showing historical trends, and pie charts are used to show comparisons of parts to a whole. Figures 10, 11, and 12 illustrate the uses of these three types of charts. The figures shown on these charts were obtained from the teller department statistics shown earlier in this chapter. The monthly teller transactions on the line chart are imaginary in part but were developed as if each month's teller department statistical report for 1978 and 1977 were available. Bar charts can also be shown horizontally. Pie charts can be revolved to suit the eye. Line charts can be shaded under the line to show more dramatically the hills and valleys. A variation of the vertical bar chart can be used to stimulate employees in reaching a goal by using one bar to create a chart resembling a thermometer. As each part of the goal is achieved, the bar is lengthened until the whole goal is accomplished.

The Power of Statistics

The following true account of what happened in a bank many years ago illustrates the power of using statistics in management. The bank was located in an urban area and had about 15,000 checking accounts—many of which had a low average monthly balance but high activity. The bank had just begun what was to be a year-long drive to increase profits. The president directed the senior officers in the various divisions to generate and implement ideas that either increased income or decreased expense.

One day the senior operations manager was describing the bank's profit improvement campaign to the manager of the bookkeeping department in an effort to solicit his help. As the discussion progressed, it centered around what the manager of

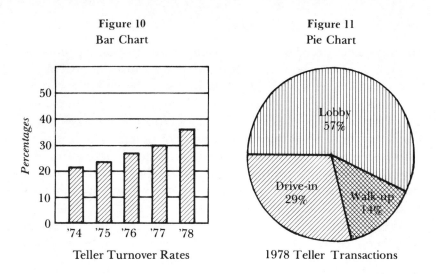

Figure 10
Bar Chart

Teller Turnover Rates

Figure 11
Pie Chart

1978 Teller Transactions

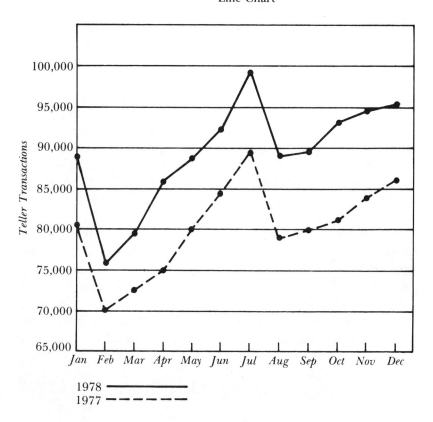

Figure 12
Line Chart

the bookkeeping department could do to increase profits. A brief discussion about decreasing expenses in the department (which yielded few ideas) was followed by a discussion about income. Both the senior operations manager and the department manager began asking each other about income items related to checking accounts. There were a lot of questions asked such as: "I wonder what the monthly service-charge income is for the different types of accounts, for overdraft charges, for returned deposited checks, etc?" Neither manager had any statistics available and, therefore, no answers.

At the next meeting a few days later, the two managers analyzed readily available service-charge income statistics which had been obtained from the control department. In reviewing these statistics they found that the income from checking-account related service charges of all types seemed low in relation to the number of accounts maintained and to the volume of checks processed. The manager of the bookkeeping department, who also had the daily responsibility of reviewing overdrawn checking accounts, knew that there was a high volume of checks returned for "insufficient funds" each day. During the meeting he happened to remark, "You know, if we increased our return check charge for overdrawn accounts by only one dollar per check we could probably increase our income a lot per month." The senior manager asked, "By how much?" After thinking a moment the bookkeeping manager answered, "well, we return probably sixty or seventy checks per working day times twenty-two working days—that's about $1300 to. $1500 per month." Both managers looked at each other in amazement.

This simple piece of statistical information about overdraft charges provided a spark that literally ignited something in the bookkeeping manager's mind. This manager, who was good at his job mainly because he was highly people-oriented, had shown no interest in or aptitude for numbers up to this point in his career. For some reason, he became intrigued with the idea of increasing income through checking-account related service-charges.

He began by keeping detailed income records for his department. No source of income was left unaccounted—business-account service charges, personal-check charges, stop payment and returned deposited-check charges, income lost from waived or rebated charges were all meticulously recorded. This statistical record-keeping motivated him to think of ways to increase income. He recommended and obtained approval to raise service-charge rates to a level more in keeping with industry-wide rates. He lobbied and was successful in having other officers in the bank charge those accounts which for years had been on a service charge-waive basis. He charged customers a per hour rate for special services performed. Month after month he recorded and reviewed his income statistics and watched the income grow and grow. The result of this one man's efforts, with the aid of statistics, increased income in this bank from checking-account related charges over $10,000 per month—$120,000 per year! This remarkable performance could not have been accomplished without the accumulation and review of statistics.

A manager need not be an experienced accountant to become proficient in developing meaningful statistical data. Statistics, for the department manager, should be simple in content and relatively easy to compile. With a minimum of effort, statistics can produce enormous benefits. They can provide motivation. They can be an aid in developing goals. In essence, statistics provide knowledge of the past with which a manager can influence the future.

VIII
Managing the Future

How can I advance in my career? is a question often asked by managers. The first chapter of this book outlined several characteristics of successful managers, and the succeeding chapters explained ways to manage others effectively. If applied, these principles will help a manager to do his job well, thus paving the way for future advancement. But advancing in one's career involves additional efforts. These efforts may be termed career management, or management of the future. What follows is an explanation of the two important components of career management which cannot be overlooked by those who seek advancement—career planning and boss relationships.

Career Planning

One of the keys to the successful management of any worthwhile endeavor is planning. Developing a career path involves planning—both long range and short range—and establishing definite career goals. A person cannot plan to arrive somewhere in his career without knowing where he wants to go anymore than he can plan how to get to a vacation resort without knowing which resort he wants to visit. Career planning first requires a goal. General goals such as earning a lot of money or having more responsibility border on mere daydreaming. Developing more specific goals is more meaningful. The process of developing specific goals requires knowledge of one's aptitudes, abilities, likes, and dislikes as they relate to work.

If a person is thinking of a future job involving the supervision of others, then he should like motivating, training, and counseling other people, and he should have the ability to relate to others in these ways. If a person wants a job making loans, then he should be interested in analyzing the financial responsibility and personal attributes of a borrower, and he should have the ability to do this. Obviously, establishing career goals requires knowledge about the specific job desired. The more one knows about the job, the more sure will be the decision to reach it, and the more motivated will be the efforts to attain it.

Once one has determined the job one wants, planning to attain that goal can begin. This always requires the acquisition of knowledge about the job through on-the-job experience combined with outside education (private reading, college-level courses, seminars, etc.). The two hypothetical examples that follow will be helpful in determining how to plan a career.

Bette Mulvaney graduated from college two years ago with a degree in economics. She took a job immediately with a large bank as a management trainee. After spending a few months in each of several departments in the bank (as part of the training program), Bette accepted a job as a credit analyst in the commercial loan department. A few months later she was promoted to supervisor of three other credit analysts. She has held this job for the past year. Bette is a career-minded person and has decided that she likes banking. She thinks that she would like to be a loan officer. To be sure about the loan officer idea, she found out more about what loan officers do by observing them at work, by asking them about their jobs, and by reading about the duties and responsibilities of a bank loan officer. The more she investigated, the more appealing the idea became. Bette then matched what she knew about loan work to her abilities and concluded that she was capable of analyzing a person's credit capabilities and of assuming responsibility for loan decisions.

Now that Bette had established a career goal for herself, she could begin to plan her activities toward attaining this goal. She proceeded to assess her education and job experience as it related to her goal and found that she was seriously lacking in knowledge about accounting, credit administration, and analyzing financial statements. She then made specific plans for courses she would take to acquire this knowledge. In order to gain some practical knowledge in making loans, Bette planned to ask management, after she had begun her educational program, if she could spend some time during her normal work week working with a loan officer. She also would ask to attend some loan officer meetings. For the time being, this completed her career planning. Bette then proceeded to implement the plan.

Twenty-seven-year-old Tom Stevenson has been a manager of the bookkeeping department of a medium-sized bank for the past three years. He is good at his job. He relates to his employees well and likes the challenge of developing better work procedures. Tom already has decided that his talents and interests center around the management of people and the functions they perform in the operations division of the bank. His goal is to acquire more and more management responsibility through the simultaneous management of several departments. Eventually Tom would like to become the cashier of the bank. In this bank the cashier has the responsibility of managing six departments—bookkeeping, proof, teller, customer service, purchasing, and personnel.

In assessing his banking background, Tom realized that he had only the limited knowledge about other operating departments that he had gained through his daily contact with them and through the few courses he had taken with the American Institute of Banking. Tom started his career development with the following plans.

Tom realized that accounting is a very basic course of study for anyone aspiring to a career in banking. Since he had had only one semester of accounting in college, he planned to take at least one more semester. Since he had no educational background in personnel work, he decided to take at least two personnel courses. Since he had only practical knowledge in supervision, he planned to take a course in management to understand more of the theory involved. Tom planned to assess the situation again after he had completed this part of his education.

Along with his outside educational activities, Tom decided to learn more on the job about the proof and teller areas of the bank. Fortunately his department, bookkeeping, was located next to the proof department and only one floor away from the teller department. Since Tom had the foresight to develop the people in his department to think for themselves and operate efficiently when he was on vacation or away from the department, he felt that he could reasonably arrange to be away from his department at least two or three hours a week to further his training in the proof and teller departments. He planned to ask his manager for her permission to proceed with this plan.

Tom Stevenson, like Bette Mulvaney, planned to develop himself on two fronts at once—through outside education and through on-the-job training. He felt that after he expanded his knowledge of other departments he would be in a better position to be promoted to the simultaneous management of more than one department or to the management of a larger department of the bank.

Both Bette and Tom have developed plans for their respective careers. They have goals in mind and are willing to take time and effort to reach these goals. Their plans create a twofold effect. They will be gaining knowledge and at the same time making a favorable impression on management. Management is always impressed with those employees who are willing to further their development by personally investing time, ingenuity, and effort.

When developing career plans, one should not be concerned with what jobs might be open in the future, but rather with being prepared when openings occur. In a growing organization there are often more openings available than there are qualified people to fill them.

There is, of course, always the possibility that, even after preparing for the future, promotional opportunities are still not presenting themselves. If this happens, an individual always has the right to ask management why. He or she has nothing to lose and everything to gain. It is important for the career-minded person to know why he or she has not been considered for advancement. If the person's immediate boss can offer no concrete answers then a manager on a higher level should be consulted.

In the final analysis, the responsibility for planning a career rests principally with the individual rather than with the organization. The organization can often provide means to help employees (such as financial assistance for educational purposes and counseling in career planning), but the planning, implementation, and completion of the project are largely dependent upon the determination and effort of the individual.

Boss Relationships

The other important component of career development is maintaining an advantageous relationship with higher management. This includes one's immediate boss and all members of management with whom one comes in contact. Members of the management team of a bank do not operate in isolation. They often communicate with each other about the abilities of those who are candidates for promotion. It is important, therefore, for those who aspire to higher levels of management to cooperate and get along with all the officers and managers of a bank.

Every supervisor has an immediate boss who judges his performance and recommends him for promotion, salary increases, additional responsibilities, etc. In career development, the single most important person in the bank is often the immediate boss. His recommendations and comments about a supervisor's abilities and performance have great influence when promotional opportunities arise. Getting along with him professionally is important.

What does a boss look for when judging a supervisor's performance? There are five important factors.

1. *Judgment.* Does the supervisor make good, commonsense decisions based on sufficient information, or does he decide in haste without analyzing the consequences? Does he have the

fortitude to make decisions, or does he avoid them by transferring the responsibility to his boss?

2. *Dependability.* Is the supervisor always on duty, or is he often absent from the department? Is he precise and timely in response to the requests of the boss for information, or does he often present his boss with inaccurate and incomplete facts? Are these responses given as soon as possible, or are they late and even forgotten?

3. *Knowledge.* Does the supervisor really know all the details about the way the department operates? How much about other departments and the banking business in general does he know? Is the supervisor knowledgeable about the latest management techniques being used, about new equipment being offered by manufacturers, about new systems and procedures being used and new services being offered by other banks?

4. *Initiative.* Is the supervisor active in trying to improve his department? Is he a pathfinder or a path follower? Does he rely on his boss to prod him along, or is he a step ahead of his boss? Does he have the spirit of accomplishment?

5. *Supervisory ability.* Is the supervisor a good manager of other people—can he organize their efforts, communicate with them effectively, train them well, and motivate them to do their jobs better?

These are the primary factors a boss considers when making a decision about the performance of a supervisor. In order for a boss to witness a supervisor's performance, he has to be in communication with him. Supervisors should not isolate themselves from their bosses, but rather should keep them posted on anything of importance that is going on in their departments, any significant accomplishments or new procedures. When necessary, the supervisor should ask his boss's advice in regard to a particularly difficult problem that has to be solved. This, however, should always be done with the understanding that the supervisor will solve the problem himself.

Bosses are human beings and so will react to situations differently. Certain minor events might irritate one boss but have little effect upon another. If the boss is irritated by certain incidents, even though minor in nature, it makes sense to be sure these incidents do not happen in the future.

Some bosses are reluctant to discuss a supervisor's performance with him—either to compliment or to criticize. If the supervisor is seriously concerned about his performance, he should question his boss. It is important for a career-minded supervisor to know how he is doing, particularly if there is some correctable performance problem which could hinder his advancement.

Salary discussions with a boss should be centered around performance rather than the supervisor's personal need for more money. A good solid performance record, accurately stated, including a list of substantial accomplishments, is the strongest argument a supervisor can use to obtain a salary increase.

For those who want a career in banking, the possibilities are limitless. Banking is a growing industry, and it will continue to grow as long as the nation and its people prosper. Within banking there is a variety of sub-professions—accounting, marketing, management of people, methods and research, personnel, credit administration, auditing, electronic data processing, international finance, trust admininstration, investments, etc. One can become an expert in any one of these fields and find the opportunity to develop a rewarding career. As in any profession, however, an individual's progress and growth are largely a result of the personal effort expended in planning and accomplishing career objectives.